Camping Tennessee

Help Us Keep This Guide Up to Date

Every effort has been made by the authors and editors to make this guide as accurate and useful as possible. However, many things can change after a guide is published—campgrounds open and close, grow and contract, regulations change, techniques evolve, facilities come under new management, etc.

We appreciate hearing from you concerning your experiences with this guide and how you feel it could be improved and kept up to date. While we may not be able to respond to all comments and suggestions, we'll take them to heart and we'll also make certain to share them with the authors. Please send your comments and suggestions to the following email address:

FalconGuides
Reader Response/Editorial Department
Falconeditorial@rowman.com

Thanks for your input, and happy camping!

Camping Tennessee

A Comprehensive Guide to the State's Best Campgrounds

Second Edition

Harold R. Stinnette
Revised by Sunshine Loveless

FALCONGUIDES

ESSEX, CONNECTICUT

FALCONGUIDES®

An imprint of Globe Pequot, the trade division of The Rowman & Littlefield Publishing Group, Inc.
4501 Forbes Blvd., Ste. 200
Lanham, MD 20706
www.rowman.com

Falcon and FalconGuides are registered trademarks and Make Adventure Your Story is a trademark of The Rowman & Littlefield Publishing Group, Inc.

Distributed by NATIONAL BOOK NETWORK

British Library Cataloging in Publication Information available

Library of Congress Cataloging-in-Publication Data

Names: Stinnette, Harold R. author. | Loveless, Sunshine, author.
Title: Camping Tennessee: a comprehensive guide to the state's best
    campgrounds / Harold R. Stinnette; revised by Sunshine Loveless.
Description: Second edition. | Essex, Connecticut: FalconGuides, [2023] |
    Summary: "Organized in three distinct sections (East Tennessee, Middle
    Tennessee, and West Tennessee), this guidebook contains detailed
    information on over 100 public campgrounds in Tennessee accessible by
    car, for tenters and RVers"— Provided by publisher.
Identifiers: LCCN 2022046873 (print) | LCCN 2022046874 (ebook) | ISBN
    9781493057955 (paperback) | ISBN 9781493057962 (epub)
Subjects: LCSH: Camping—Tennessee—Guidebooks. | Camp sites, facilities,
    etc.—Tennessee—Directories. | Tennessee—Guidebooks.
Classification: LCC GV191.42.T2 S75 2023 (print) | LCC GV191.42.T2
    (ebook) | DDC 796.5409768—dc23/eng/20221013
LC record available at https://lccn.loc.gov/2022046873
LC ebook record available at https://lccn.loc.gov/2022046874

♾™ The paper used in this publication meets the minimum requirements of American National Standard for Information Sciences—Permanence of Paper for Printed Library Materials, ANSI/NISO Z39.48-1992.

The authors and The Rowman & Littlefield Publishing Group, Inc., assume no liability for accidents happening to, or injuries sustained by, readers who engage in the activities described in this book.

Contents

I would like to thank my wife, Michelle, for her support, encouragement, and willingness to go on crazy adventures with me. She makes everything more fun and anything possible. I would like to acknowledge the Native Lands of: **ᏣᎳᏊ** *Tsalaguwetiyi (Cherokee, East), S'atsoyaha (Yuchi), Shawandasse Tula (Shawanwaki/ Shawnee), and Chikashsha* Ịyaakni' *(Chickasaw). These tribes inhabited colonial Tennessee before the Indian Removal Act of 1830 which allowed the US government to forcibly remove them from their native lands (source: Native-land.ca).*

Introduction

Tennessee is affectionately known as the Volunteer State and is synonymous with country music, Elvis Presley, Dolly Parton, and the Great Smoky Mountains. Even in our modern society, it's a place where you'll still find Southern charm and hospitality pouring from the hearts and souls of the people that call this state home. One visit to Chattanooga was all it took to hook me and convince me to move to Tennessee. Part of the lure was the kindness of the people I met; the other was the rugged, natural beauty of eastern Tennessee. After moving to Chattanooga twenty-one years ago, it is now the place I call home. My introduction to camping and the outdoors came as a child living in California, but it was absent in my teens living in Kansas. After moving to Tennessee and working as a raft guide on the Ocoee River in my 20s, I was reintroduced to the outdoors as both a lifestyle and a way to make a living. Today, my wife and I go camping as often as possible to escape the stress of modern life and reconnect with nature. It was such a joy doing research for this book by participating in a hobby that I truly enjoy with a newfound sense of purpose.

Tennessee's landscape, people, and history are diverse, from the plains of west Tennessee to the Cumberland Plateau in Middle Tennessee to the Appalachian Mountain range of East Tennessee. Great Smoky Mountains National Park is the most biodiverse park in the National Park System. The more than 800 square miles of the park contain more than 19,000 documented species. Tennessee has been inhabited by a variety of people throughout centuries, from Native Americans to European colonizers to white settlers, and today is a melting pot of diversity thanks in part to its low cost of living, lack of state income tax, universities, and manufacturing and tourism industries.

I would like to acknowledge the Native Lands of GWJ♈ᎮᎫᏏ Tsalaguwetiyi (Cherokee, East), S'atsoyaha (Yuchi), Shawandasse Tula (Shawanwaki/Shawnee) and Chikashsha Iyaakni' (Chickasaw) that inhabited colonial Tennessee before the Indian Removal Act of 1830 that allowed the US government to forcibly remove Indians from their native lands (source: Native-land.ca). As they were rounded up and led on the Trail of Tears to Oklahoma, not only did they lose their homes, many lost their lives. To this day, no tribal lands exist in Tennessee, despite the great presence of the Cherokee people and history in east Tennessee.

Tennessee has fifty-six state parks, thirty-six of which have campgrounds. The parks tend to feature such natural attractions as lakes, mountains, and waterfalls, and camping at one of these parks is the best way to explore nature without going too remote. Whether you like RV camping, pitching a tent, or staying in rustic cabins during your commune with nature, Tennessee state parks have it all.

Upper East Tennessee mountains

Weather

Tennessee has a humid, subtropical climate with hot and humid summers and mild to cold winters. Summers are hot and humid in Tennessee, with the average daily temperatures above 90°F. Nights tend to be mild, with temperatures near 70°F. Winters range from mild to cold, with average low temperatures ranging from 22°F to 33°F during the month of January. Higher elevations are colder than the plains, but freezing temperatures occur in much of the state. Spring is warm and wet with comfortable temperatures but sees the frequent passage of storms including tornadoes. Autumn is relatively dry, and the conditions are pleasant. Tennessee receives generous precipitation that averages more than 50 inches annually. Rainfall is throughout the year, with the wettest period between December and April and the driest between August and October. Midsummer sees ample rainfall in much of the state, especially in the high mountains. The best time to visit Tennessee is during the fall season from mid-September to mid-November, when the summer humidity and temperatures drop. The day highs tend to be between 65°F and 73°F in October, while the nights are pleasant. Fall colors tend to peak by the fourth week of October and remain through mid-November. The worst time to visit is in January and February, when the winter weather is at its coldest and wettest. Be sure to check local weather conditions using your favorite weather app before heading out on your camping trip and often while traveling, as weather conditions can change suddenly and unexpectedly in the region.

Flora and Fauna

With its varied terrain and soils, Tennessee has an abundance of flora, including at least 150 kinds of native trees. Tulip tree (the state tree), shortleaf pine, and chestnut, black, and red oaks are commonly found in the eastern part of the state, while the Highland Rim abounds in several varieties of oak, hickory, ash, and pine. Gum maple, black walnut, sycamore, and cottonwood grow in the west, and cypress is plentiful in the Reelfoot Lake area. In East Tennessee, rhododendron, mountain laurel, and wild azalea blossoms create a blaze of color in the mountains. More than 300 native Tennessee plants, including foxglove and ginseng, have been utilized for medicinal purposes.

Recreation

Outdoor enthusiasts of all types will find their style of outdoor play in Tennessee. The Great Smoky Mountains is a hiker's paradise offering more than 800 miles of hiking trails. East Tennessee is home to some of the best whitewater rivers and creeks in the United States, including the Ocoee and Hiwassee Rivers. Mountain biking has become incredibly popular throughout Tennessee, with extensive trail systems in the Cherokee National Forest and many state parks. Chattanooga is a mecca for rock climbers, with more rock to climb within a 25-mile radius than Boulder, Colorado, has to offer. With 1,393 lakes in the state, flatwater paddling options abound along with ample opportunities to fish or cool off in a natural swimming hole.

How to Use This Guide

This book is divided into three sections: East Tennessee, Middle Tennessee, and West Tennessee. Directions are listed with each campground, with starting points at the closest town or other major points of interest. In most cases there are several ways to reach each campground; the best route really depends on where you're coming from. There is road signage for most campgrounds and state parks across the state, and most of the directions go with their signage. In addition to the maps and directions contained in this book, I also recommend utilizing a GPS system to help you navigate the back roads of Tennessee.

An "at a glance" chart at the beginning of each area provides a quick reference to what each campground has to offer. In the chart you'll find basic information such as operating season, number of sites, hookups, fees, and recreational activities available in the area. Because some information, like season and fees, may change from year to year, a phone number is included for each campground so you can call for more information. Within the description of each campground, you'll find additional information on what the area around the campground has to offer.

Everyone experiences the outdoors differently and has different camping styles. We hope this book offers insight and helps connect you with the campgrounds that fit your style and allow you to create lasting memories.

Key

Hookups: W = Water   E = Electric   S = Sewer
Toilets: F = Flush   V = Vault   C = Chemical
H = Hiking
S = Swimming
F = Fishing
B = Boating
L = Boat launch
R = Horseback riding
O = Off-roading
W = Wildlife watching
M = Mountain biking
P = Paddling
C = Rock climbing
G = Golf
Cell service: none, spotty, good
Maximum Trailer/RV length given in feet
Stay limit given in days

Campground Fee Ranges (per night)

$ = $0–$10
$$ = $11–$20
$$$ = $21–$30
$$$$ = $31 and above

Overview of Camping in Tennessee

Camping is a simple way to connect with the natural world, and this book is intended to help connect you with the public camping options in Tennessee. We're here to help you dream up your next trip, figure out the details, and reserve experiences at 116 facilities with over 7,400 individual campsites across the state of Tennessee. There's something for everyone in this guide, so get out there, have an adventure, and bring home a story!

The campgrounds covered in this guide are public, meaning they are owned and operated by a state park, national park, municipality, or some other government organization. These are not the only campgrounds in Tennessee. There are hundreds of privately owned camping facilities that readers can access through other guidebooks or the internet.

Seven agencies oversee public campgrounds in Tennessee: the National Park Service, the USDA Forest Service (USFS), state parks, city or county parks, the Tennessee Valley Authority (TVA), and the US Army Corps of Engineers. Each agency provides visitors with quality campgrounds. These agencies are listed below with a brief description of the type of campground they manage, information on what they offer, and any regulations that apply to their campgrounds.

National Park Service

The National Park Service in Tennessee manages Great Smoky Mountains National Park (GSMNP), Big South Fork National Recreation Area, and the Obed Wild and Scenic River. All three of these areas offer some type of camping. Two of the campgrounds in the Great Smoky Mountains on the Tennessee side—Elkmont and Cades Cove—accept reservations; the other three are on a first-come, first-served basis. Reservations are taken for both campgrounds in Big South Fork. The Obed Wild and Scenic River is primarily a kayaking and canoeing area with limited camping facilities. The Smokies and Big South Fork offer a variety of historic and recreational opportunities. The National Park Service offers annual and lifetime America the Beautiful—National Parks and Federal Recreational Lands Passes for US residents to purchase to access federal lands. Holders of the Senior and Access Passes can receive a 50 percent discount for single family campsites at GSMNP, Big South Fork, TVA, and some USFS campgrounds.

USDA Forest Service

The US Department of Agriculture Forest Service (USFS) oversees three areas that offer public camping in Tennessee: Cherokee National Forest—Northern Districts,

Cherokee National Forest—Southern Districts, and Land Between the Lakes. Some of the best wildlands in the state fall under the jurisdiction of the USFS. The campsites in these districts vary from basic with no amenities to "the works" RV camping. While there is no general admission fee to the national forests, some areas do have small access fees. Visit fs.usda.gov/cherokee for more information.

State Parks

Tennessee's state park system is one of the best in the country, offering free access to all fifty-six parks across the state. Thirty-six of the fifty-six state parks offer camping facilities. Tennessee seniors, age 62 and older, receive a 25 percent discount on all campsites in Tennessee state parks. You can find out more about all Tennessee state parks at tnstateparks.com/; for campground information, check tnstateparks.com/lodging/campgrounds.

City or County Parks

These campgrounds are either managed by a city government or under a county jurisdiction. Very few public campgrounds are run by local governments, and their amenities and conditions vary more than those of any other agency. These facilities usually are directly managed by an individual who lives on the property and handles everything from mowing the grass to collecting camping fees.

Tennessee Valley Authority

The Tennessee Valley Authority (TVA) offers hundreds of campsites among its six dam reservoir campgrounds in Tennessee. All six campgrounds are now managed by Recreation Resource Management (RRM) under a concessionaire agreement with TVA. This has allowed an expansion of services that includes new campground stores, wireless access, an online reservation system, and more. (TVA also owns several campgrounds that are not listed in this book because they have been leased to private individuals.) For more information about TVA campgrounds or other river and lake information, visit tva.com/environment/recreation/camping.

US Army Corps of Engineers

All Corps campgrounds in Tennessee are located in Middle Tennessee. The campgrounds managed by this agency are a pleasure to visit, in most part due to the campground hosts. Campground hosts at each Corps campground are managed by an outside vendor; this creates a uniform system from campground to campground. The website for reservations (recreation.gov) has maps of the campgrounds along with a list of what's available.

Zero-Impact Camping—Leave No Trace

A successful camping trip with family and friends can provide great memories for years to come. A truly successful trip has a positive outcome for both the camper and the environment. Leaving your camping area with zero impact on the environment and no detectable sign of your presence is a great compliment to your camping abilities. Zero impact doesn't just happen, however; you must prepare for it. Use the following guidelines before, during, and at the end of your camping trip to help ensure that the trip is a success for both you and the environment.

Plan for success. The fact that you are using a guidebook is a good start. Before camping in a new area, it's always a good idea to check the weather and camping conditions ahead of time. Preparing for the weather—for example, knowing that rain is in the forecast for that region—helps in planning what to take. You'll need to know if there are any special regulations for that camping area. For example, is it bear habitat? Are there any special food storage regulations? Having a plan for meals each day, and packing your food according to that plan, can minimize the amount of trash that must be disposed of. Make a packing list, and double-check to make sure you don't forget any essential items—or carry things you don't need. Some campgrounds are very popular and fill to capacity during peak seasons, so plan ahead by making a reservation where possible or getting to the campground early.

Camp only in designated areas. Most campgrounds have tent pads and paved RV sites. These are provided to minimize the impact on the areas around the campsites. Several campgrounds in Tennessee have strict rules concerning where to place tents and RVs; not adhering to these rules can result in a stern warning, a fine—even expulsion. When hiking or even walking from the bathhouse, stay on established paths. Doing this lessens the impact of erosion and reduces the number of unauthorized trails cutting across and through campgrounds.

Pack it in; pack it out. The old camping rule "pack it in, pack it out" is still a good one and should be followed whenever camping in an area that has no place to dispose of waste. All the public campgrounds listed in this book provide trash receptacles. Most of the state park and national park campgrounds have containers for both trash and recyclables. Recycle aluminum and plastic whenever possible, and encourage others to do the same. Never throw leftovers from a meal on the ground around the campsite or into the fire ring; this encourages wildlife to come into the site looking for an easy meal. Either dispose of leftovers in the trash container or store them in a secure vehicle for later disposal. Many campgrounds offer utility sinks for cleaning dishes. If sinks are provided, use them; avoid washing dishes in streams or lakes.

Take only pictures; leave only footprints. One of the reasons we camp is to be outdoors and enjoy the beauty of nature. Preserving what we find and leaving it behind allows others the same joy. Leave rocks, plants, and natural areas as you found them.

Build campfires sensibly. Sitting around a campfire at night is great joy for both young and old, but before lighting your fire, check with a ranger or campground host for fire regulations and conditions. If a fire ring is provided, use it. Resist the urge to build really large fires. A fire that is too big can easily get out of control. Never throw cans or glass into the fire ring; these items will not burn, and they cause an unsightly mess. Never leave a fire unattended, and whenever you leave the campsite, be sure the fire is completely out.

Camp in harmony with wildlife. Observe wildlife from a distance. If you are camping with a pet, be sure to keep it under control. Never let your pet chase or harass wildlife. Remember: It's their home—you're just visiting.

Be a good camping neighbor. Courtesy is contagious, so spread it around. Respect other campers by keeping noise levels and voices low. Quiet hours are established in most campgrounds; make yourself aware of the rules, and don't run motors or generators during quiet hours. Take only the space that is designated for your campsite; if you're not sure whether part of the site is yours or your neighbor's, be courteous and let the other site use the space. If you need the space, be considerate and ask first. Camping with your pet can be a positive experience, but keep in mind that a barking dog is a nuisance to other campers.

Following these simple guidelines will help make your camping trip a more enjoyable experience for everyone. Camping in a socially and environmentally responsible way encourages others to follow suit—and will go a long way to ensure that future generations also have a place to camp.

Interacting with Our Environment

One reason to camp is the joy of being outdoors and experiencing nature firsthand. We all love to view wildlife up close, hike a beautiful mountain trail, or see that first wildflower bloom in spring. But along with this experience comes responsibility. Camping memories can be made more special when we take the time to enjoy nature in a positive and meaningful way. Appreciation of our natural world and the things that share this world with us is a value to be learned and shared with all who enjoy being outdoors. Those of us who fit into this category should hold an extra level of respect for the environment we share.

Wildlife
Respect wildlife. Wildlife and campers often share the same territory. It's always a great experience to see a wild animal in its natural habitat, and bringing home a good memory can be made easier by following a few guidelines.

Never approach wildlife too closely. Each state or national park has a set of guidelines for how close is too close, but as a rule, if you're close enough to make an animal change its behavior, then you're probably too close. All wildlife can be dangerous if it feels threatened—no matter if it's a black bear or a chipmunk. Always give extra room to a mother animal and her young, and never back an animal into a corner—always leave an escape route for both you and the animal.

Feeding wildlife is strongly discouraged. This can lead a wild animal to become a "panhandler" and puts both the animal and you in danger. Animals that are accustomed to being fed are more likely to be harmed by the food than helped. Human food, especially snack food, is often high in sugar, preservatives, and many other ingredients that are harmful to wild animals. In addition, people are often bitten by animals they are feeding—the animal doesn't realize where the food stops and the hand begins.

In the Great Smoky Mountains and the Cherokee National Forest of East Tennessee, special consideration must be taken for camping in black bear habitat. Food storage is one of the main considerations. Food should be stored in a secure area, preferably a hard-sided camper, RV, or vehicle. Never store food or anything that smells like food in a tent. Please ask when checking in at one of the campgrounds in these areas about bears and proper food storage.

Wildflowers

Each spring visitors flock to parks and natural areas to search out spring wildflowers. The spring bloom is a highly anticipated event every year and is becoming more and more a tradition among family and friends. One tradition that needs to be broken, however, is gathering wildflowers, either to plant in a personal wildflower garden or use as a bouquet for the dining room table. It is illegal to gather or pick wildflowers in national parks. The wildflowers in our parks and sanctuaries are protected for everyone to enjoy, and when a wildflower is picked, its beauty is taken from everyone else who visits that park. Many wildflowers dug up for personal gardens end up dying because they do not transplant well. Over-picking and over-gathering have led to several wildflowers being protected by law as endangered.

Many of the parks in Tennessee hold annual wildflower pilgrimages where experts on the subject share their knowledge. This is a great way to interact with nature in a positive way. There are many local guidebooks on the subject of wildflowers; pick one up to take on your wildflower walks. By learning the names of wildflowers and the areas in which they grow, your knowledge and respect for them will also grow.

Trees

When camping during the heat of summer, you can really appreciate the shade provided by a large tree. It is very important when camping in a forested area not to damage the trees in the campground. A tree's bark is its skin, and damaging or breaking that skin allows disease and infection to penetrate the tree, which can lead to its death.

Never hammer nails or other sharp objects into trees. Always remove any rope or line that has been tied to a tree. Many campgrounds allow gathering firewood from the surrounding area as long as the wood is dead and downed. Never cut firewood from a live tree.

Firewood is often available from campground stores or nearby convenience stores. Plenty of shade in a campground is always a plus, and working together we can protect our trees and ensure that future generations will have them to enjoy.

Hiking

Time spent hiking and exploring the forest can be an enjoyable part of your camping trip. Hiking is a great form of exercise and is also a way to slip a little further back into the seclusion of the wilderness. Always check trail conditions before heading out. Most campground hosts or park rangers have updated information on trails and trail conditions.

Many hiking trails in Tennessee cover some pretty steep territory, switching back and forth as they climb steep ridge sides. Always stay on the trail; this is both for your safety and to protect the trail. Taking shortcuts at switchbacks wears a second path. Often this path is straight down, which can lead to water runoff and trail erosion. When hiking, always pack out what you carry in. It is very disconcerting to hike for some time to an out-of-the-way destination—only to find someone's garbage left behind.

It's Our Responsibility

Our environment, parks, and natural areas are ours to protect and cherish. They are ours to enjoy today and preserve for future generations. As the saying goes: "Our natural lands do not belong to us; we are merely borrowing them from our children." Keeping this in mind every time you are camping and enjoying the outdoors will help ensure that your memories are positive ones.

LEGEND

40	Interstate Highway	● 1	Camp Locator
27	US Highway	🌲	Wilderness Area
29	State Highway	⛺	Campground
———	Road	ⓘ	Visitor Center
—·—·—	State Border	Gatlinburg ○	Town
▬▬▬	Park Boundary	■	Structure/Point of Interest
~~	River/Dam		Scale
	Lake		

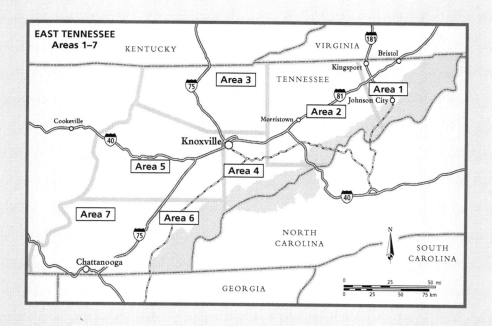

Area 1: Bristol, Johnson City, and Kingsport

These cities, located in the northeast corner of Tennessee, are nicknamed "the Tri-Cities." All three are modest-size cities with a small-town feel. Here the traveler can find everything from car racing to art museums to college basketball games. Most of this area is surrounded by the Cherokee National Forest, and between the national forest and Tennessee state parks, there are more than 400 individual campsites.

For more information:
Kingsport Chamber of Commerce
400 Clinchfield St. #100
Kingsport 37660
(423) 392–8800
kingsportchamber.org

Bristol Tennessee/Virginia Chamber of Commerce
20 Volunteer Pkwy.
Bristol 37620
(423) 989–4850
bristolchamber.org

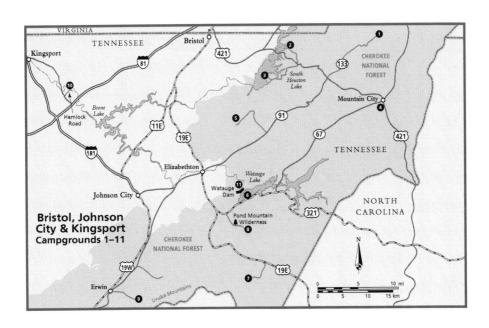

Campground number	Campground	Group Sites	RV Sites	Total Sites	Max RV Length	Hookups	Toilets	Showers	Drinking water	Dump station	Pets	ADA Sites	Recreation	Fees ($)	Season	Can reserve	Stay limit (days)
1	Backbone Rock			10			FV		•	•	•	•	HSFMW	$-$$	Apr–Oct	•	14
2	Jacobs Creek		15	29	30 ft	WE	FV	•	•	•	•	•	HSFBLP	$$	Apr–Oct	•	14
3	Little Oak		69	69	30 ft	WE	FV	•	•	•	•	:	HSFBLP	$$	Apr–Oct	•	14
4	Johnson County Welcome Center Campground		14	14	40 ft	WES	F	•	•	•	•			$$$	Apr–Oct	•	None
5	Low Gap			5			V				•	•	HW		Mar–Oct		14
6	Carden's Bluff		2	43	30 ft		F	•	•	•	•	•	HSFBLPW	$$	Apr–Oct	•	14
7	Roan Mountain State Park	4	86	106	89 ft	WE	F	•	•	•	•	•	HSFW	$$–$$$$		•	28
8	Dennis Cove	1	13	15	30 ft		F	•	•	•	•	•	HSFMW	$-$$	Apr–Oct	•	14
9	Rock Creek	1	27	32	48 ft	WE	F	•	•	•	•	•	HSFW	$$–$$$$	May–Oct	•	14
10	Warrior's Path State Park	2	94	99	40 ft	WE	F	•	•	•	•	•	HSFBLPMW	$$–$$$$		•	28
11	Watauga Dam Campground		29	29	40 ft	WES	F	•	•	•	•	•	HSFBLPW	$$–$$$$	Mar–Nov	•	21

Hookups: W = Water   E = Electric   S = Sewer

Toilets: F = Flush   V = Vault   C = Chemical

Recreation: H = Hiking   S = Swimming

F = Fishing   B = Boating   L = Boat launch   R = Horseback riding   O = Off-road driving   W = Wildlife watching   M = Mountain biking

C = Rock climbing   G = Golf   P = Paddling

If no entry under Season, campground is open all year. If no entry under Fee, camping is free.

Campground Fee Ranges (per night): $=$10 or less $$=$11–$20 $$$=$21–$30 $$$$=$31 and above

1 Backbone Rock, Cherokee National Forest

Location: East of Bristol
GPS coordinates: 36.596818 / -81.818840
Facilities and amenities: Fire rings, grills, tent pads, picnic tables; flush and vault toilets; centrally located water
Elevation: 2,100 feet
Road conditions: Paved
Hookups: None
Sites: 10
Maximum RV length: N/A
Season: Apr–Dec
Fee: $-$$
Maximum stay: 14 days
Management: Cherokee National Forest, Watauga Ranger District; (423) 753-1500
Reservations: recreation.gov/camping/campgrounds/251757
Pets: Yes
Quiet hours: 10 p.m.–6 a.m.
ADA compliant: Yes
Cell service: None
Activities: Hiking, fishing, mountain biking, rappelling, swimming. The trailhead for the Appalachian National Scenic Trail (#1) is approximately 0.25 mile south of the campground on TN 133. Damascus, Virginia is approximately 5 minutes north of the campground, offering access to mountain bike trails.
Finding the campground: From Bristol, travel south on US 421 for 20 miles to Shady Valley. Turn left onto TN 133 for 8 miles to the recreation area. After passing through the tunnel at Backbone Rock, look for the campground entrance on the left.
About the campground: Backbone Rock Campground is a small campground located adjacent to TN 133. Backbone Rock Recreation Area, named for a unique rock formation, is just south of the campground. At the turn of the twentieth century, the railroad drilled a tunnel through the ridge for logging trains to pass through. On weekends the "World's Shortest Tunnel" is a popular place for rappelling. A short trail will take the adventurous to the top of Backbone Rock. Beaverdam Creek flows through the recreation area and is stocked with trout by the Tennessee Wildlife Resources Agency (TWRA).

2 Jacobs Creek, Cherokee National Forest

Location: East of Bristol on South Holston Lake

GPS coordinates: 36.563498 / -82.003892

Facilities and amenities: Picnic tables, fire rings, lantern posts; centrally located water and showers; flush toilets; dump station. The bathhouse in Loop B is ADA accessible.

Elevation: 1,730 feet

Road conditions: Paved to gravel

Hookups: WE

Sites: 29

Maximum RV length: 30 feet

Season: Apr–Oct

Fee: $$

Maximum stay: 14 days

Management: Cherokee National Forest, Watauga Ranger District; (423) 735-1500

Reservations: recreation.gov/camping/campgrounds/10128487

Pets: Yes

Quiet hours: 10 p.m.–6 a.m.

ADA compliant: Yes

Cell service: Good

Activities: Fishing, paddling, water sports, swimming, hiking

Finding the campground: From Bristol, take US 421 south for 12 miles; turn left onto paved Denton Valley Road. Travel 2 miles and turn left onto paved Jacobs Creek Road. This road becomes gravel 0.9 mile from the campground.

Tunnel through Backbone Rock Recreation Area

About the campground: This campground, situated on a peninsula on South Holston Lake in the Jacobs Creek Recreation Area, is a great spot for summer water activities. The campground has a large beach area with plenty of grass for picnicking. A public boat launch is located about 0.5 mile west on US 421. South Holston Lake is a favorite summer destination for fishing enthusiasts, pleasure boaters, and water-skiers. The area also offers a shooting range about 1 mile from the campground. A 15-mile self-guided auto tour on FR 87 provides an educational experience on how the Cherokee National Forest is managed.

3 Little Oak

Location: East of Bristol
GPS coordinates: 36.515497 / -82.049376
Facilities and amenities: Fire rings, picnic tables, lantern posts; showers, flush and vault toilets; centrally located water; dump station
Elevation: 1,900 feet
Road conditions: Paved to gravel
Hookups: WE
Sites: 69
Maximum RV length: 30 feet
Season: Apr–Oct
Fee: $$
Maximum stay: 14 days
Management: Cherokee National Forest, Watauga Ranger District; (423) 753-1500
Reservations: recreation.gov/camping/campgrounds/122240
Pets: Yes
Quiet hours: Unknown
ADA compliant: Yes
Cell service: Spotty
Activities: Boating, water-skiing, fishing, hiking, wildlife watching
Finding the campground: From Bristol, follow US 421 South for 12 miles and turn right onto Camp Tom Howard Road. After 0.5 mile the road becomes gravel FR 87. Follow FR 87 for 6 more miles; turn right onto FR 87G and follow it 1.5 miles to the campground.
About the campground: Little Oak sits on the edge of South Holston Lake. Most campsites have a view of Holston Lake, and several allow access to the lake from the campsite. The lake offers many recreational activities, including boating, water-skiing, and fishing, but the area is also loaded with hiking opportunities. There are a couple of short trails in the recreational area and several in the surrounding areas of Holston Mountain. This area has been designated as a Watchable Wildlife Area. Early morning and late afternoon are good times to see such wildlife as white-tailed deer and wild turkeys.

4 Johnson County Welcome Center Campground

Location: Near downtown Mountain City
GPS coordinates: 36.467432 / -81.803732
Facilities and amenities: Showers, flush toilets; dump station; water, sewer, and electric hookups
Elevation: 2,400 feet
Road conditions: Paved
Hookups: WES
Sites: 14
Maximum RV length: 40 feet
Season: Apr–Oct
Fee: $$$
Maximum stay: No limit
Management: Johnson County Welcome Center; (423) 727-5800
Reservations: johnsoncountytnchamber.org/area-info/tourism-campground/
Pets: Yes; limit 2 dogs per campsite
Quiet hours: Unknown
ADA compliant: No
Cell service: Good
Activities: Hiking; shopping in Mountain City
Finding the campground: The welcome center is located on US 421 in Mountain City; the campground is directly behind the welcome center.
About the campground: This campground is better suited for RVs but does offer tent camping in an open field. The campground is located just behind the welcome center and about 3 blocks from downtown antiquing. Mountain City is a quaint mountain town that has made a revival of its mountain history. Hiking is available in nearby Cherokee National Forest.

5 Low Gap, Cherokee National Forest

Location: North of Elizabethton
GPS coordinates: 36.441203 / -82.124569
Facilities and amenities: Picnic tables, fire rings, lantern post; vault toilets
Elevation: 3,900 feet
Road conditions: Paved to gravel
Hookups: None
Sites: 5
Maximum RV length: N/A
Season: Mar–Oct
Fee: free
Maximum stay: 14 days
Management: Cherokee National Forest, Watauga Ranger District; (423) 735-1500
Reservations: No; first come, first served
Pets: Yes
Quiet hours: 10 p.m.–6 a.m.
ADA compliant: No
Cell service: Spotty
Activities: Hiking
Finding the campground: From Elizabethton, take TN 91 North for 7 miles. Turn left onto FR 56 and go 4 miles to a fork in the road; take the left fork onto FR 202 and continue 3 miles to the campground. *Caution:* Low-clearance vehicles will not be able to make the drive in on the gravel road.
About the campground: Low Gap is a very primitive camping area with limited campsites and amenities. This is a good spot to get away from the crowds and enjoy some peace and quiet.

6 Cardens Bluff, Cherokee National Forest

Location: North of Hampton
GPS coordinates: 36.310810 / -82.116231
Facilities and amenities: Tables, grills, lantern posts; flush toilets, showers; centrally located water
Elevation: 2,000 feet
Road conditions: Paved
Hookups: None
Sites: 43
Maximum RV length: 30 feet
Season: Apr–Oct
Fee: $$
Maximum stay: 14 days
Management: Cherokee National Forest, Watauga Ranger District; (423) 735-1500
Reservations: recreation.gov/camping/campgrounds/122390
Pets: Yes
Quiet hours: 10 p.m.–6 a.m.
ADA compliant: Yes
Cell service: Good
Activities: Water sports, paddling, fishing, swimming, hiking, biking, wildlife viewing
Finding the campground: From Hampton, take US 321 South/TN 67 East 4.1 miles to the entrance of Cardens Bluff Campground; turn left at the sign.
About the campground: Overlooking 6,430-acre Watauga Lake, Cardens Bluff is a ridgetop campground with spectacular views. The campsites are at various heights on the ridge—sites at the top afford views of the lake; others are at the water's edge. There is a boat ramp 1 mile west on US 321; Shook Branch Swim Area, on the shores of Watauga Lake, is also nearby. Hiking is available on the Cardens Bluff Trail, which starts at the campground, as well as in nearby Cherokee National Forest.

7 Roan Mountain State Park

Location: Southeast of Elizabethton
GPS coordinates: 36.159305 / -82.100123
Facilities and amenities: Tables, grills, lantern posts; centrally located water, showers; dump station
Elevation: 6,285 feet
Road conditions: Paved
Hookups: WE
Sites: 106; 86 with water and electric hookups
Maximum RV length: 89 feet
Season: Apr–Nov; self-contained RVs year-round
Fee: $$–$$$$
Maximum stay: 28 days
Management: Roan Mountain State Park; (423) 772-0190
Reservations: reserve.tnstateparks.com/roan-mountain
Pets: Yes
Quiet hours: 10 p.m.–6 a.m.
ADA compliant: Yes
Cell service: Good
Activities: Hiking, swimming, fishing

View from an overlook at Roan Mountain

Finding the campground: Take TN 19E south out of Elizabethton and travel 17 miles to the town of Roan Mountain. Turn right onto TN 143 and go 2 miles to the park; the campground is another 2 miles past the visitor center.

About the campground: Roan Mountain State Park has much to offer. It is most famous for the 600-acre natural rhododendron garden atop Roan Mountain. Peak bloom is near the end of June each year, and the park holds a Rhododendron Festival that coincides with the bloom. (***Note:*** Camping here is first come, first served, and the campground fills quickly during the festival.) The Appalachian Trail (AT) crosses Roan Mountain at Carver's Gap, and there are good day hiking opportunities on the AT from the campground. The Doe River runs through the park, offering trout fishing in season.

8 Dennis Cove, Cherokee National Forest

Location: East of Hampton
GPS coordinates: 36.256824 / -82.110699
Facilities and amenities: Tables, grills, lantern posts, fire rings; flush and vault toilets; centrally located water
Elevation: 2,650 feet
Road conditions: Paved
Hookups: None
Sites: 15
Maximum RV length: 30 feet
Season: Apr–Oct
Fee: $–$$
Maximum stay: 14 days
Management: Cherokee National Forest, Watauga Ranger District; (423) 735-1500
Reservations: recreation.gov/camping/campgrounds/251724
Pets: Yes
Quiet hours: 10 p.m.–6 a.m.
ADA compliant: Yes
Cell service: None
Activities: Hiking, swimming, fishing, mountain biking
Finding the campground: From Hampton and US 321/TN 67, turn right at Citizens Bank onto Dennis Cove Road; travel 5.1 miles to the Dennis Cove Recreation Area and the campground.
Caution: This is a very steep, narrow road with several switchbacks.
About the campground: Dennis Cove Campground is nestled back in a secluded cove, with more of a wilderness feeling than some other campgrounds in the national forest. The campsites are located next to Laurel Creek, a small stream that is stocked with trout. Not far from the campground is Laurel Creek Lodge, a haven for Appalachian Trail hikers. Campers from Dennis Cove can also find limited supplies and a shower at the lodge for a small price. Hiking opportunities are numerous in the Dennis Cove Recreation Area. Laurel Fork Trail (#39) follows the creek upstream for 8.0 miles with twenty-six stream crossings. The Appalachian National Scenic Trail is accessed via the nearby Coon Den Falls Trail (#37). There is no garbage pickup in the area, so you must pack out what you packed in.

⑨ Rock Creek, Cherokee National Forest

Location: East of Erwin
GPS coordinates: 36.138018 / -82.350374
Facilities and amenities: Tables, fire rings, lantern posts; centrally located flush toilets, showers, and water; dump station; water hookups; 11 sites with electric hookups; stream-fed swimming pool
Elevation: 2,300 feet
Road conditions: Paved
Hookups: WE
Sites: 32
Maximum RV length: 48 feet
Season: May–Oct
Fee: $$–$$$$
Maximum stay: 14 days
Management: Cherokee National Forest, Nolichucky/Unaka Ranger District; (423) 638-4109
Reservations: recreation.gov/camping/campgrounds/267551
Pets: Yes
Quiet hours: 10 p.m.–6 a.m.
ADA compliant: Yes
Cell service: Spotty
Activities: Hiking, biking, fishing, paddling, swimming, whitewater rafting
Finding the campground: From Main Street in Erwin, take TN 395 East for 3.5 miles to the Rock Creek Recreation Area; the entrance to the campground is on the left.
About the campground: Camping here is like stepping back in time; most of the facilities were built by the Civilian Conservation Corps (CCC) in the 1930s and still retain the feel of yesteryear. The USDA Forest Service constructed the campground in the 1960s. This large recreation area is a great spot to beat the summer heat. The swimming pool is fed by a small stream that forks off Rock Creek. The campground has two large double sites with electric hookups and enough room for two large RVs. Flush toilets, showers, and water are centrally located. Several hiking trails and an easy bike trail are located in the Rock Creek Recreation Area.

10 Warrior's Path State Park

Location: East of Kingsport
GPS coordinates: 36.497451 / -82.479358
Facilities and amenities: Tables, grills; flush toilets, showers; dump station; 94 sites with water and electric hookups
Elevation: 883 feet
Road conditions: Paved
Hookups: WE
Sites: 99
Maximum RV length: 40 feet
Season: Some sites year-round
Fee: $$-$$$$
Maximum stay: 28 days
Management: Warrior's Path State Park; (423) 239-7141
Reservations: reserve.tnstateparks.com/warriors-path
Pets: Yes
Quiet hours: 10 p.m.–6 a.m.
ADA compliant: Yes
Cell service: Good
Activities: Fishing, swimming, biking, boating, paddling, hiking, horseback riding, golf
Finding the campground: From I-81, take exit 59 and travel north onto TN 36. Turn right onto Hemlock Road; follow signs to the park entrance.
About the campground: Warrior's Path is named for an ancient warpath used by the Cherokee Indians. The park sits on the shores of Fort Patrick Henry Reservoir and the Holston River, so boating, water-skiing, and fishing are among the many activities available here. The large campground is a great base for a family weekend or a short vacation. With hiking and mountain biking trails, horseback riding, boating, and an eighteen-hole golf course, this campground offers something for everyone in the family. Canoes, pontoon boats, and paddleboats can be rented at the marina. If you bring your own, slips can be rented to store your boat. Points to visit outside the park include Bays Mountain Nature Center and Appalachian Caverns.

11 Watauga Dam Campground (TVA)

Location: East of Johnson City
GPS coordinates: 36.333737 / -82.125800
Facilities and amenities: Tables, grills; flush toilets, showers; dump station; 29 sites with water and electric hookups, 3 with sewer; store
Elevation: 1,959 feet
Road conditions: Paved
Hookups: WES
Sites: 29
Maximum RV length: 40 feet
Season: Mar–Nov
Fee: $$–$$$$
Maximum stay: 21 days
Management: Tennessee Valley Authority; (423) 543-0233
Reservations: camprrm.com/parks/tennessee/tva-6/watauga-dam-campground/
Pets: Yes
Quiet hours: 10 p.m.–7 a.m.
ADA compliant: Yes
Cell service: Spotty
Activities: Fishing, swimming, boating, paddling, hiking
Finding the campground: From TN 321 in Elizabethton, go south on TN 19E and then turn onto TN 91 toward Hunter. Go about 3 miles; turn right onto Blue Springs Road at the stoplight by the Citgo Station. Follow the road, keep to the right, and cross two bridges. Turn right immediately after crossing the second bridge, then right at the end of the road.
About the campground: Watauga Dam Campground is a beautiful, peaceful campground on the Watauga River in eastern Tennessee. Currently the campground has no tent sites but has twenty-nine RV sites, many of which are right on the river. All RV sites have electric service and water; three sites have sewer connections as well. Water activities are most popular here.

Area 2: Morristown and Greeneville

Morristown and Greeneville are historic towns in East Tennessee. In fact, founded in 1783, Greeneville is the second-oldest town in Tennessee. Downtown Greeneville has a plethora of antiques shops and galleries and is home to the Andrew Johnson National Historic Site. In Morristown you'll find the Crockett Tavern, owned by Davy Crockett's parents and where he spent most of his boyhood. The town's architecture is interesting and showcases a second-story sidewalk. Walkways above the downtown sidewalk are accessible by ramps and lead to stores that are on the "second floor." Both towns sit at the foothills of the Appalachian Mountains just outside the Cherokee National Forest and in close proximity to Douglas Dam and Reservoir, which offers 513 miles of shoreline along the French Broad River.

For more information:
Morristown Area Chamber of Commerce
PO Box 9
Morristown 37815
(423) 586-6382
morristownchamber.com

Greene County Partnership/Chamber
115 Academy St.
Greeneville 37743
(423) 638-4111
discovergreenevilletn.com

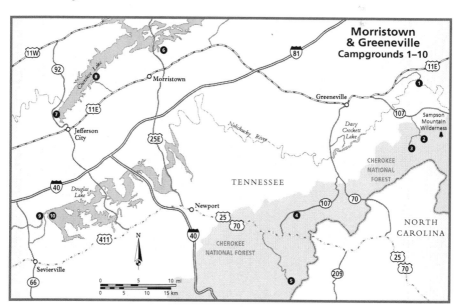

Campground number	Campground	Group Sites	RV Sites	Total Sites	Max RV Length	Hookups	Toilets	Showers	Drinking water	Dump station	Pets	ADA Sites	Recreation	Fees ($)	Season	Can reserve	Stay limit (days)
1	David Crockett Birthplace State Park	1	54	88	65 ft	WES	F	•	•	•	•	•	HSFPW	$$-$$$$		•	14-28
2	Horse Creek			15			FV	•	•		•			HSFW	$	May–Oct		None
3	Old Forge			10			V							HSRW	$	May–Oct		None
4	Houston Valley			8	20 ft		F			•	•			HW	$	Mar–Dec		None
5	Round Mountain			14			V		•	•	•			HW	$	May–Nov		None
6	Cherokee Park		74	74	40 ft	WES	F	•	•	•	•		•	HSFBLPW	$$$			None
7	Cherokee Dam Campground		39	44	40 ft	WE	F	•	•	•	•	•	•	HSFBLPW	$$-$$$$	Mar–Nov	•	21
8	Panther Creek State Park		50	50	66 ft	WES	F	•	•	•	•	•	•	HSFBLPWM	$$$		•	28
9	Douglas Dam Tailwater		58	61	50 ft	WE	F	•	•	•	•	•	•	HSFBLPW	$$-$$$$	Mar–Nov	•	21
10	Douglas Dam Headwater		54	60	50 ft	WE	F		•	•	•	•	•	HSFBLPW	$-$$$$	Mar–Nov	•	21

Hookups: W = Water   E = Electric   S = Sewer

Toilets: F = Flush   V = Vault   C = Chemical

Recreation: H = Hiking   S = Swimming   F = Fishing   B = Boating   L = Boat launch   R = Horseback riding   O = Off-road driving   W = Wildlife watching   M = Mountain biking
C = Rock climbing   G = Golf   K = Paddling

If no entry under Season, campground is open all year. If no entry under Fee, camping is free.

Campground Fee Ranges (per night): $=$10 or less $$=$11–$20 $$$=$21–$30 $$$$=$31 and above

1 David Crockett Birthplace State Park

Location: Northeast of Greeneville
GPS coordinates: 36.209350 / -82.658600
Facilities and amenities: Grills, tables; flush toilets, showers; dump station; water and electric hookups; 54 sites with sewer hookups; swimming pool
Elevation: 1,420 feet
Road conditions: Paved
Hookups: WES
Sites: 88
Maximum RV length: 65 feet
Season: Open year-round
Fee: $$–$$$$
Maximum stay: 14–28 days
Management: David Crockett Birthplace State Park; (423) 257-2167
Reservations: reserve.tnstateparks.com/david-crockett-birthplace
Pets: Yes
Quiet hours: 10 p.m.–6 a.m.
ADA compliant: Yes
Cell service: Good
Activities: Swimming, fishing, paddling, hiking, wildlife viewing
Finding the campground: From Greeneville take US 11E North for approximately 10 miles. Turn right onto South Heritage Road (Old Route 34); go 1.2 miles and turn right onto Davy Crockett Road. Travel another 1.2 miles; Davy Crockett Road makes a sharp right curve and joins Keebler Road. From here it is 0.9 mile to the entrance to Davy Crockett Birthplace State Park.
About the campground: The campground here has a very basic layout—situated on a flat piece of land not far from the Nolichucky River. It is open, with only part of the campground having large trees for shade. The campground sites could be improved by adding grills and fire rings. Some sites are on the banks of the river, and there is river access for anyone wishing to fish. The interesting thing here is the history. The park and its facilities pay tribute to Davy Crockett, legendary frontier hero. The park's museum tells the story of his life, and there is a replica of the log cabin where Davy was born on the banks of the Nolichucky River.

2 Horse Creek, Cherokee National Forest

Location: East of Greeneville
GPS coordinates: 36.107970 / -82.657122
Facilities and amenities: Tables, fire rings, lantern posts; flush and vault toilets; centrally located water
Elevation: 1,720 feet
Road conditions: Paved
Hookups: None
Sites: 15
Maximum RV length: N/A
Season: May–Oct
Fee: $
Maximum stay: No limit
Management: Cherokee National Forest, Nolichucky/Unaka Ranger District; (423) 638-4109
Reservations: No; first come, first served
Pets: Yes
Quiet hours: 10 p.m.–6 a.m.
ADA compliant: No
Cell service: None
Activities: Hiking, fishing, swimming
Finding the campground: From Tusculum in Greeneville, take TN 107 North for 6.5 miles. Turn right onto Horse Creek Road and go 2.5 miles to the campground entrance.
About the campground: This is a beautiful campground located just inside the Cherokee National Forest and the foothills of the Appalachian Mountains. Large hemlock trees shade most of the campground, and Horse Creek flows through the middle of the area. From May 15 to October 15, only disabled persons, children under the age of 12, and seniors are allowed to fish in the section of Horse Creek that runs through the recreation area. There are several hiking trails in the nearby Sampson Mountain Wilderness.

Paved walkway to swimming and picnic area at Horse Creek

3 Old Forge, Cherokee National Forest

Location: East of Greeneville
GPS coordinates: 36.092364 / -82.682930
Facilities and amenities: Fire rings, tables, lantern posts; vault toilets; tent-only sites; horse corral next to the camping area; no potable water
Elevation: 1,870 feet
Road conditions: Dirt road, rough
Hookups: None
Sites: 10
Maximum RV length: N/A
Season: May–Oct
Fee: $
Maximum stay: No limit
Management: Cherokee National Forest, Nolichucky/Unaka Ranger District; (423) 638-4109
Reservations: No; first come, first served
Pets: No
Quiet hours: 10 p.m.–6 a.m.
ADA compliant: No
Cell service: None
Activities: Horseback riding, hiking, fishing, swimming
Finding the campground: From Greeneville, take TN 107 East (off US 11E) for 6 miles and then follow signs to Horse Creek Recreation Area (approximately 2 miles). From Horse Creek, turn right onto FR 331 for 3 miles. The road dead-ends at the campground.

Scenic overlook at Jennings Creek, Old Forge Campground

About the campground: Old Forge is a secluded, quiet area to camp. Located at the dead end of FR 331, it's a peaceful place to spend a weekend. The entire campground has walk-in tent sites only, but they are a short distance from the parking area. Each site is very well marked off, with a large area to pitch a tent. All sites are wheelchair accessible, but the restrooms do not meet ADA requirements. Old Forge is a great destination for equestrians, having more than 8 miles of horse trails. Jennings Creek, which flows along the edge of the campground, is a good place to fish, wade, swim, or relax.

4 Houston Valley, Cherokee National Forest

Location: South of Greeneville
GPS coordinates: 35.965102 / -82.942781
Facilities and amenities: Tables, fire rings, lantern posts; 2 flush toilets shared by the campground and picnic area; no potable water
Elevation: 1,800 feet
Road conditions: Paved road to campground; gravel in campground
Hookups: None
Sites: 8
Maximum RV length: 20 feet
Season: Mar–Dec
Fee: $
Maximum stay: No limit
Management: Cherokee National Forest, Nolichucky/Unaka Ranger District; (423) 638-4109
Reservations: No; first come, first served
Pets: Yes
Quiet hours: 10 p.m.–6 a.m.
ADA compliant: No
Cell service: None
Activities: Hiking, wildlife viewing; nearby rifle range
Finding the campground: From Greeneville, take TN 70 South for 10 miles. Turn right onto TN 107 West and go 9 miles; Houston Valley campground is on the left.
About the campground: Houston Valley is a small campground and picnic area located just a few yards off TN 107. While this is more of a primitive campground with unimproved sites, the sites are spaced out with plenty of room between them. Most of the sites are on a slight hillside. USDA Forest Service information indicates that seven of the sites can accommodate 20-foot trailers. The Weaver Bend Watchable Wildlife Area is located nearby, as well as many hiking trails.

5 Round Mountain, Cherokee National Forest

Location: South of Greeneville
GPS coordinates: 35.838601 / -82.953856
Facilities and amenities: Tables, fire rings, lantern posts; vault toilets
Elevation: 3,100 feet
Road conditions: Gravel, very narrow and winding
Hookups: None
Sites: 14
Maximum RV length: N/A
Season: May–Nov
Fee: $
Maximum stay: No limit
Management: Cherokee National Forest, Nolichucky/Unaka Ranger District; (423) 638-4109
Reservations: No; first come, first served
Pets: Yes
Quiet hours: 10 p.m.–6 a.m.
ADA compliant: No
Cell service: None
Activities: Hiking, wildlife viewing; wildflower viewing in spring
Finding the campground: From Greeneville, take TN 70 South for 10 miles. Turn right onto TN 107 and travel 13 miles. Turn right onto US 25/70 and go 3 miles; turn left on TN 107. From here, follow signs to the campground.

Hamblen County Marina, next to Cherokee Park Campground

About the campground: This is a very remote, secluded campground. If your idea of camping is getting away to a more quiet area, this would be a good choice. With an elevation of approximately 3,100 feet, it is also one of the highest-elevation campgrounds in the Cherokee National Forest. The two most popular things to do here are hiking and wildflower viewing. There are several locations for the hiker to access the Appalachian Trail, and Max Patch—a popular destination for viewing wildflowers—is near here.

⑥ Cherokee Park

Location: Morristown
GPS coordinates: 36.258623 / -83.274048
Facilities and amenities: Pavilions and shelters; showers, flush toilets; dump station; electric and water hookups; children's wading pool, 2 playgrounds, volleyball courts, boat ramp
Elevation: 1,000 feet
Road conditions: Paved
Hookups: WES
Sites: 74
Maximum RV length: 40 feet
Season: Year-round
Fee: $$$
Maximum stay: No limit
Management: Hamblen County; (423) 586-0325
Reservations: No; first come, first served
Pets: Yes
Quiet hours: 10 p.m.–6 a.m.
ADA compliant: Yes
Cell service: Spotty
Activities: Fishing, picnicking, disc golf, volleyball, water sports, paddling
Finding the campground: From Morristown take US 25E; go 2.3 miles and turn right onto Cherokee Park Road. Go 0.2 mile; the entrance to Cherokee Park is on the left.
About the campground: Cherokee Park is a 178-acre public park on the banks of Cherokee Lake offering picnic pavilions, a championship eighteen-hole disc golf course, public restrooms, an amphitheater, a boat launch area, a marina, a splash pad, and children's playground areas. Cherokee Lake is well known for its year-round fishing opportunities, and this family-oriented campground has plenty of amenities to entertain kids of all ages. A nearby boat dock provides boat launching, rental boats, and concessions.

7 Cherokee Dam Campground

Location: Southwest of Morristown
GPS coordinates: 36.154872 / -83.514715
Facilities and amenities: Tables, grills; showers, flush toilets; centrally located water; dump station; boat launch, beach area
Elevation: 1,082 feet
Road conditions: Paved
Hookups: WE
Sites: 44
Maximum RV length: 40 feet
Season: Mar–Nov
Fee: $$–$$$$
Maximum stay: 21 days
Management: Tennessee Valley Authority; (865) 361-2151
Reservations: camprrm.com/parks/tennessee/tva-6/cherokee-dam-campground/
Pets: Yes
Quiet hours: 10 p.m.–6 a.m.
ADA compliant: Yes
Cell service: Spotty
Activities: Fishing, boating, paddling, water-skiing, swimming, nature trails
Finding the campground: From Jefferson City, head west on 11E, then right on 92N, and go 4.8 miles to the "Dam & Campground" entrance. From I-40, take exit 417 to TN 92; follow it north to the Dam & Campground entrance. *Caution:* From New Market, we highly advise not turning onto Mill Springs Road if towing or driving a camper/fifth wheel due to the low freeway overpass.
About the campground: TVA'S Cherokee Dam Campground is located in Jefferson City on the upstream side of the Cherokee Dam. The campground has a total of forty-four campsites, with four sites being ADA accessible. All campsites are equipped with water and electricity except for five primitive tent-only sites on the eastern front end of the lake. Nearly every campsite in the campground has a view of the beautiful lake and mountains. The entry roads into the campground are paved, and most campsites are level with gravel parking pads. Each campsite has a picnic table and fire pit/grill. In the center of the campground, two bathhouses provide hot showers and flush toilets. Other recreational opportunities near the campground include swimming, boating, and hiking. The easy Cherokee Cross Country Trail provides spectacular views of Cherokee Lake and Cherokee Dam.

8 Panther Creek State Park

Location: West of Morristown
GPS coordinates: 36.214802 / -83.405176
Facilities and amenities: Tables, grills, lantern posts, fire rings; showers, flush toilets; dump station and laundromat; electric and water hookups; swimming pool, playgrounds
Elevation: 1,460 feet
Road conditions: Paved
Hookups: WES
Sites: 50
Maximum RV length: 66 feet
Season: Mar–Nov; some camping available year-round, but with no water
Fee: $$$
Maximum stay: 28 days
Management: Panther Creek State Park; (423) 587-7046
Reservations: reserve.tnstateparks.com/panther-creek
Pets: Yes
Quiet hours: 10 p.m.–6 a.m.
ADA compliant: Yes
Cell service: Good
Activities: Boating, fishing, swimming, paddling, mountain biking, hiking, horseback riding, volleyball, tennis, horseshoes
Finding the campground: From Morristown take US 11E south to TN 342W. Turn right onto TN 342W and travel 2.3 miles to the entrance to Panther Creek State Park.
About the campground: Panther Creek State Park is a 1,444-acre park located on the Cherokee Reservoir in the historic Holston River Valley. The park has seventeen hiking trails covering more than 30 miles of terrain at all levels of difficulty. Hikers can enjoy magnificent views of Cherokee Lake and the Cumberland Mountains from Point Lookout Trail. There are also more than 15 miles of mountain biking trails, ranging from easy to difficult.

⑨ Douglas Dam Tailwater

Location: North of Sevierville
GPS coordinates: 35.957428 / -83.549203
Facilities and amenities: Tables, fire rings; showers, flush toilets; electric and water hookups at some sites; boat launch, playground
Elevation: 853 feet
Road conditions: Paved
Hookups: WE
Sites: 61
Maximum RV length: 50 feet
Season: Mar–Nov
Fee: $$–$$$$
Maximum stay: 21 days
Management: Tennessee Valley Authority; (865) 361-1522
Reservations: camprrm.com/parks/tennessee/tva-6/douglas-tailwater-campground/?it=parks/douglas-tailwater-campground/
Pets: Yes
Quiet hours: 10 p.m.–6 a.m.
ADA compliant: Yes
Cell service: Spotty
Activities: Boating, fishing, paddling, relaxing
Finding the campground: From TN 66 in Sevierville, take TN 338 North for 6 miles; the entrance to the campground is on the right.
About the campground: Fishing seems to be the big draw to this campground on the banks of the French Broad River. There are sixty-one sites here divided into two sections by the road that runs through the campground. One section is on the banks of the river; the other section is across the road. A stay limit of twenty-one days is strictly enforced on the riverside, but after the twenty-one days, you can move your camp to the other section. This campground and the Douglas Dam Headwater Campground could be good places to stay if you are visiting one of the tourist towns of Pigeon Forge or Sevierville.

10 Douglas Dam Headwater

Location: North of Sevierville
GPS coordinates: 35.957338 / -83.535656
Facilities and amenities: Tables, grills; showers, flush toilets; centrally located water; dump station; water and electric hookups; boat launch, beach area
Elevation: 915 feet
Road conditions: Paved
Hookups: WE
Sites: 60
Maximum RV length: 50 feet
Season: Mar–Nov
Fee: $$-$$$$
Maximum stay: 21 days
Management: Tennessee Valley Authority; (865) 361-1379
Reservations: camprrm.com/parks/tennessee/tva-6/douglas-headwater-campground/
Pets: Yes
Quiet hours: 10 p.m.–6 a.m.
ADA compliant: Yes
Cell service: Mostly good
Activities: Fishing, boating, water-skiing, swimming, nature trails
Finding the campground: From TN 66 in Sevierville, take TN 338 North for 4.2 miles. Turn right onto Boat Launch Road and go 1 mile; the campground entrance is on the right.

Campsite on the shore of Douglas Lake, Douglas Dam Headwater

About the campground: Douglas Dam Headwater is above the dam, as we would say, meaning that it is next to the lake created by the dam. Here you will find plenty of open water for just about any water activity you can think of. Some campsites are on the shore, and some are on a hill over-looking the lake. Boats can be moored at several of the lakeside sites. According to the TVA office, the stay limit here is thirty days, but some sites are available for long-term rental.

Area 3: Norris and Big South Fork

Norris, Tennessee, started out as a planned community for the workers constructing Norris Dam. The original town plan was adopted from England's garden city movement of the 1890s—the buildings and houses were built on smaller lots with large open areas known as commons. The original houses were built from twelve basic designs, and today you can still see many of these first buildings. The town has grown but has maintained its roots as a family-friendly community.

The Big South Fork National River and Recreation Area was set aside to protect this section of the Cumberland Plateau's natural beauty and to provide economic growth from recreation instead of coal mining and timber cutting. The area is maintained by the National Park Service and provides such outdoor activities as kayaking, canoeing, rafting, hiking, mountain biking, horseback riding, hunting, and fishing. The 125,000-acre recreation area is shared by Tennessee and Kentucky.

For more information:
Big South Fork National River and
Recreation Area
(Bandy Creek Visitor Center)
4564 Leatherwood Rd.
Oneida 37841
(423) 286-7275
nps.gov/biso

Anderson County Chamber of
Commerce
245 North Main St., Ste. 200
Clinton 37716
(865) 457-2559
andersoncountychamber.org

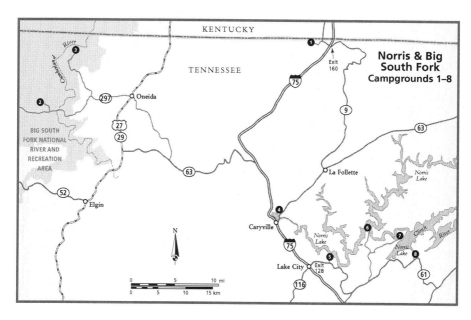

Campground number	Campground	Group Sites	RV Sites	Total Sites	Max RV Length	Hookups	Toilets	Showers	Drinking water	Dump station	Pets	ADA Sites	Recreation	Fees ($)	Season	Can reserve	Stay limit (days)
1	Indian Mountain State Park		47	47	72 ft	WES	F	•	•	•	•	•	HSFW	$$$$	Apr-Nov	•	28
2	Bandy Creek	2	96	181	50 ft	WE	F	•	•	•	•	•	HSPFRM	$$-$$$$		•	14
3	Station Camp Horse Camp		20	24	32 ft	WE	F		•	•	•	•	HRW	$$$		•	14
4	Cove Lake State Park		100	106	50 ft	WE	F	•	•	•	•	•	HSFBLPW	$$$		•	28
5	Norris Dam State Park		55	85	56 ft	WE	F	•	•	•	•	•	HSFBLPWM	$$-$$$		•	Varies
6	Anderson County Park	1	50	63	40 ft	WE	F	•	•	•	•	•	HSFBLPWM	$$-$$$		•	21
7	Loyston Point	1	59	64	42 ft	WE	F	•	•	•	•	•	HSFBLPW	$$$-$$$$	Mar-Nov	•	21
8	Big Ridge State Park	1	45	50	35 ft	WE	F	•	•	•	•	•	HSFBLPW	$-$$$	Apr-Nov	•	28

Hookups: W = Water   E = Electric   S = Sewer

Toilets: F = Flush   V = Vault   C = Chemical

Recreation: H = Hiking   S = Swimming   F = Fishing   B = Boating   L = Boat launch   R = Horseback riding   O = Off-road driving   W = Wildlife watching   M = Mountain biking

C = Rock climbing   G = Golf   P = Paddling

If no entry under Season, campground is open all year. If no entry under Fee, camping is free.

Campground Fee Ranges (per night): $=$10 or less $$=$11-$20 $$$=$21-$30 $$$$=$31 and above

1 Indian Mountain State Park

Location: Near the town of Jellico
GPS coordinates: 36.587032 / -84.140869
Facilities and amenities: Tables, grills, fire rings; showers, flush toilets; dump station; electric and water hookups; swimming pool
Elevation: 918 feet
Road conditions: Paved
Hookups: WES
Sites: 47
Maximum RV length: 72 feet
Season: Apr–Nov; camping allowed year-round, but no water after Nov 1
Fee: $$$$
Maximum stay: 28 days
Management: Indian Mountain State Park; (423) 566-5870
Reservations: reserve.tnstateparks.com/indian-mountain
Pets: Yes
Quiet hours: 10 p.m.–6 a.m.
ADA compliant: Yes
Cell service: Good
Activities: Swimming, fishing, pedal boats, wildlife watching, hiking
Finding the campground: From I-75 in Jellico, take exit 160 and go north on US 25 to TN 297. Make a right onto London Street and a left onto Dairy Street to the park entrance; watch for park signs.
About the campground: This is a very well-kept campground not far from Jellico, Tennessee, and the Kentucky state line. The unique feature here is that this campground and state park is developed on a reclaimed strip mine. The park has a small lake for fishing, and pedal boats are available to rent. There are walking trails around the lake and along the creek. This park is also a good place for wildlife watching, which is best in the early morning and late afternoon.

2 Bandy Creek, Big South Fork National River and Recreation Area

Location: West of Oneida
GPS coordinates: 36.488460 / -84.697342
Facilities and amenities: Tables, fire rings, lantern poles; showers, flush toilets; dump station; electric and water hookups; horse stables, swimming pool
Elevation: 1,542 feet
Road conditions: Paved
Hookups: WE
Sites: 181
Maximum RV length: 50 feet
Season: Year-round
Fee: $$–$$$$
Maximum stay: 14 days
Management: Big South Fork National River and Recreation Area, National Park Service; (423) 286-8368
Reservations: recreation.gov/camping/campgrounds/232506?tab=info
Pets: Yes
Quiet hours: 10 p.m.–6 a.m.
ADA compliant: Yes

Horse stables near Bandy Creek Campground, Big South Fork National River and Recreation Area

Cell service: Spotty

Activities: Hiking, horseback riding, mountain biking, swimming, canoeing and kayaking, fishing, rock climbing

Finding the campground: From Oneida take TN 297 West for 5 miles. TN 297 bears left and becomes TN 297-Leatherwood Ford Road. Continue for 7.2 miles; the entrance road is on the right. Watch for signs. (*Caution:* Parts of this road are very steep and curvy.)

About the campground: Bandy Creek is a spacious and modern campground situated in the Big South Fork National River and Recreation Area—a vast and scenic expanse of land that offers visitors countless recreational activities. It's very clean and well kept, and the sites are nicely spaced with plenty of room. Most sites are shaded. Big South Fork has two major draws: horseback riding and kayaking. There are stables very near the campground for those wishing to board their horses while camping at Bandy Creek. The stables offer easy access to the area's extensive trail system. Big South Fork has long been known for exciting whitewater canoeing and kayaking. The area has several streams with varying degrees of difficulty, from beginner to very advanced whitewater. Fishing is also a popular activity here.

3 Station Camp Horse Camp, Big South Fork National River and Recreation Area

Location: West of Oneida
GPS coordinates: 36.546251 / -84.636054
Facilities and amenities: Tables, lantern poles, grills; showers, flush toilets; water and electric hookups; tie-outs for 4 horses per site
Elevation: 1,443 feet
Road conditions: Paved; gravel in campground
Hookups: WE
Sites: 24
Maximum RV length: 32 feet
Season: Year-round
Fee: $$$
Maximum stay: 14 days
Management: Big South Fork National River and Recreation Area, National Park Service; (423) 569-9778
Reservations: recreation.gov/camping/campgrounds/10004358
Pets: Yes
Quiet hours: 10 p.m.–6 a.m.
ADA compliant: Yes

Campers preparing dinner at Station Camp Horse Camp, Big South Fork National River and Recreation Area

Cell service: Poor to none

Activities: Horseback riding, kayaking and canoeing, hiking, rock climbing

Finding the campground: From Oneida take TN 297 West for 5 miles. Turn right onto Station Camp Road and go 4.1 miles; the campground entrance is on the right.

About the campground: This campground was planned and built with the true horse lover in mind. Your horse can be tied out right next to your campsite. The tie-outs are well planned, with a tray to hold horse feed at head level. A concrete slab where the horse stands makes cleanup easier. The sites are large, with enough room for very large horse trailers.

4 Cove Lake State Park

Location: Caryville
GPS coordinates: 36.311752 / -84.212663
Facilities and amenities: Grills, tables; showers, flush toilets; dump station; water and electric hookups; park restaurant, playground
Elevation: 1,049 feet
Road conditions: Paved
Hookups: WE
Sites: 106
Maximum RV length: 50 feet
Season: Year-round
Fee: $$$
Maximum stay: 28 days
Management: Cove Lake State Park; (423) 566-9701
Reservations: reserve.tnstateparks.com/cove-lake
Pets: Yes
Quiet hours: 10 p.m.–6 a.m.
ADA compliant: Yes
Cell service: Good
Activities: Swimming, paddleboats, fishing, biking, tennis, volleyball, hiking, wildlife watching
Finding the campground: Cove Lake State Park is located within the city limits of Caryville. From I-75 take exit 134 to US 25W in Caryville. The entrance to the park is 0.8 mile from I-75.
About the campground: Cove Lake's 717 acres are situated in a beautiful mountain valley on the eastern edge of the Cumberland Plateau. Scenic nature trails lead through a diversity of wetlands and woodlands offering wildlife viewing for the nature enthusiast. A paved walking/biking trail provides easy access to all park facilities.

Fishing from wildlife viewing tower, Cove Lake State Park

5 Norris Dam State Park

Location: Northeast of Lake City
GPS coordinates: 36.221841 / -84.083005
Facilities and amenities: Tables, grills, lantern poles; centrally located water; showers, flush toilets; dump station; swimming pool, marina, playgrounds
Elevation: 1,410 feet
Road conditions: Paved
Hookups: WE
Sites: 85 in two camping areas
Maximum RV length: 56 feet
Season: Apr–Oct; some sites open year-round
Fee: $$–$$$
Maximum stay: 14 days (peak), 28 days (offseason)
Management: Norris Dam State Park; (865) 425-4500
Reservations: reserve.tnstateparks.com/norris-dam
Pets: Yes
Quiet hours: 10 p.m.–6 a.m.
ADA compliant: Yes
Cell service: Good
Activities: Swimming, boating, water-skiing, fishing, hiking
Finding the campground: From I-75 near Lake City, take exit 128 onto US 441; follow signs 3 miles to the park entrance.

RVs at Norris Lake, Big Ridge State Park

About the campground: Norris Dam State Park's campgrounds are divided into two areas, an east campground and a west campground. The east campground is mostly tent sites with some hookups, as well as a primitive camping area. All sites in the west campground have electrical and water hookups. The park is located on the shores of Norris Lake and has great fishing, boating, and water sport activities. Norris Dam was one of the first dams built by the Tennessee Valley Authority. But this is not the only history here. Your visit should include a stop at the eighteenth-century gristmill, the historic threshing barn, and the W. G. Lenoir Pioneer Museum.

6 Anderson County Park

Location: Andersonville
GPS coordinates: 36.286851 / -84.029852
Facilities and amenities: Tables, grills; flush toilets, showers; dump station; electric and water hookups; playground
Elevation: 1,049 feet
Road conditions: Paved
Hookups: WE
Sites: 63
Maximum RV length: 40 feet
Season: Year-round
Fee: $$–$$$
Maximum stay: 21 days
Management: Anderson County, park office; (865) 494-9352
Reservations: Anderson County, park office; (865) 494-9352
Pets: Yes
Quiet hours: 10 p.m.–6 a.m.
ADA compliant: Yes
Cell service: Good
Activities: Boating, fishing, water-skiing, swimming, walking trails
Finding the campground: From I-75 take exit 122 at Norris onto TN 61 East. Go 3.8 miles and turn left onto Park Lane; stay on Park Lane 7.3 miles into Anderson County Park.
About the campground: This really nice park is run by the local government of Anderson County. The campground is located on Norris Lake, and several sites allow you to have your boat moored right at the campsite. There is a boat launch very near the campground and also a beach area and playground, with a very large grassy area for sunbathing. There is a twenty-one-day camping limit, but site rental by the month is available. There are 6 miles of hiking/biking trails around the camping area and some very neat rock formations to explore.

7 Loyston Point

Location: North of the town of Norris
GPS coordinates: 36.267301 / -83.968008
Facilities and amenities: Tables, grills, fire rings, tent pads, lantern posts; showers, flush toilets; centrally located water; dump station; electric hookups; boat launch, beach
Elevation: 1,017 feet
Road conditions: Paved
Hookups: WE
Sites: 64
Maximum RV length: 42 feet
Season: Mar–Nov
Fee: $$$–$$$$
Maximum stay: 21 days
Management: Tennessee Valley Authority; (865) 494-9369
Reservations: camprrm.com/parks/tennessee/tva-easements/loyston-point-campground/
Pets: Yes
Quiet hours: 10 p.m.–6 a.m.
ADA compliant: Yes
Cell service: Spotty
Activities: Boating, fishing, water-skiing, water sports, swimming, hiking
Finding the campground: From I-75, take exit 122 at Norris onto TN 61 East. Go 3.8 miles and turn left onto Park Lane; continue 3.7 miles and turn right onto Forgety Road. Go 0.6 mile; Forgety Road ends at Mill Creek Road. Turn left onto Mill Creek Road and continue 0.8 mile; turn right onto a road with no road sign. Go 0.1 mile and turn left onto Loyston Point Road, where there's a sign for the campground; follow this road 2.8 miles to the campground entrance.
About the campground: Loyston Point is located on Norris Lake. The campground has several sites next to the water; all sites are within walking distance of the lake. Boats can be moored at the lakeside campsites. This seems to be a popular destination for locals on the weekend, with the swimming beach being a big draw. There is a nearby boat ramp with lots of parking available. The sites not on the water enjoy views of the lake, and several are very shaded. This is a good location for any kind of water activity.

8 Big Ridge State Park

Location: Northeast of Norris
GPS coordinates: 36.242311 / -83.930690
Facilities and amenities: Tables, grills; showers, flush toilets; dump station; water and electric hookups; beach, playground, boat launch
Elevation: 1,037 feet
Road conditions: Paved
Hookups: WE
Sites: 50
Maximum RV length: 35 feet
Season: Apr–Nov; some sites open year-round, but the bathhouse is closed.
Fee: $–$$$
Maximum stay: 28 days
Management: Big Ridge State Park; (865) 992-5523
Reservations: reserve.tnstateparks.com/big-ridge
Pets: Yes
Quiet hours: 10 p.m.–6 a.m.
ADA compliant: Yes
Cell service: Good
Activities: Fishing, paddling, boating, swimming, hiking, tennis, ball fields, playground
Finding the campground: From I-75 near Norris, take exit 122 and go east on TN 61 for 11.9 miles. Turn left onto Big Ridge Road; this is the entrance to the park.
About the campground: Part of this park's campground is on Norris Lake, but very few sites are actually on the water—and they fill early. On the other side of the park is Cove Lake; it is dammed off Norris Lake, forming a private lake for Big Ridge State Park. No private boats are allowed here, but canoes, rowboats, and paddleboat rentals are available.

Area 4: Great Smoky Mountains National Park

The Smokies, as they are known by locals and lovers of the park, comprise the country's most visited national park. It is within one day's drive of more than half the nation's population. However, this is not the only reason the Smokies are so popular. With more than a half-million acres of natural beauty, the Smokies can boast several impressive facts. The park is an International Biosphere Reserve, has more tree species than all of Northern Europe, counts for half the old-growth forest in the United States, and contains more wildflower species than any other national park in the country.

If you enjoy hiking, the park has more than 800 miles of trails, including trails for horseback riding and part of the Appalachian Trail. The park is home to miles and miles of clear mountain streams, great for both trout fishing and swimming on a hot summer day. Wildlife watching is also a great pastime here. White-tailed deer and black bears are two of the favorite animals to be seen in the park, but many more make the Smokies their home. Cades Cove is the most popular place for wildlife watching but is also a great area for bicycle riding, horseback riding, auto touring, learning about history, or just relaxing. There is no admission fee to this national park, so come on in and enjoy the mountains.

Note: Beginning March 1, 2023, there is a fee for parking anywhere within the park boundaries. However, frontcountry campers parked at their designated campsite are not required to have a parking tag. For more information visit nps.gov/grsm/planyourvisit/fees.htm#.

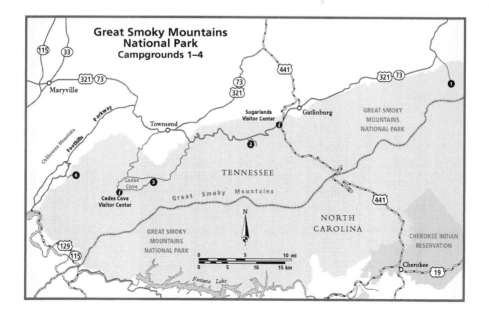

For more information:
Great Smoky Mountains National Park
107 Park Headquarters Rd.
Gatlinburg 37738
(865) 436-1200
nps.gov/grsm

Campground number	Campground	Group Sites	RV Sites	Total Sites	Max RV Length	Hookups	Toilets	Showers	Drinking water	Dump station	Pets	ADA Sites	Recreation	Fees ($)	Season	Can reserve	Stay limit (days)
1	Cosby	3	22	157	25 ft	WE	F	•	•	•	•	•	HWF	$$	Apr–Oct	•	14
2	Elkmont	4	200	220	35 ft	WE	F	•	•	•	•	•	HWFS	$$$	Mar–Nov	•	14
3	Cades Cove	4	158	159	40 ft	WE	F	•	•	•	•	•	HWR	$$$		•	14
4	Abrams Creek		16				F		•		•		HWF	$$	May–Oct	•	14

Hookups: W = Water   E = Electric   S = Sewer

Toilets: F = Flush   V = Vault   C = Chemical

Recreation: H = Hiking   S = Swimming   F = Fishing   B = Boating   L = Boat launch   R = Horseback riding   O = Off-road
driving   W = Wildlife watching   M = Mountain biking   C = Rock climbing   G = Golf   P = Paddling

If no entry under Season, campground is open all year. If no entry under Fee, camping is free.

Campground Fee Ranges (per night): $=$10 or less $$=$11-$20 $$$=$21-$30 $$$$=$31 and above

1 Cosby

Location: The northern tip of the park

GPS coordinates: 35.753572 / -83.209252

Facilities and amenities: Tables, grills, fire rings, lantern posts, tent pads; flush toilets; centrally located drinking water; dump station; river and creek access, trailheads, food storage locker

Elevation: 2,460 feet

Road conditions: Paved

Hookups: WE

Sites: 157

Maximum RV length: Under 25 feet

Season: Apr–Oct

Fee: $$

Maximum stay: 14 days

Management: Great Smoky Mountains National Park; (423) 436-1230; campground inquiries: (423) 487-2683

Reservations: recreation.gov/camping/campgrounds/232479

Pets: Yes

Quiet hours: 10 p.m.–6 a.m.

ADA compliant: Yes

Cell service: None

Activities: Hiking, fishing, wildlife watching

Finding the campground: From Gatlinburg take US 321 North for 18.2 miles. At the stop sign turn right onto TN 32 South and go 1.2 miles; turn right onto Cosby Park Road and follow it 2.1 miles to the campground.

About the campground: Tucked in the mountains under a canopy of cool shade, this campground creates a peaceful and secluded environment for visitors to Great Smoky Mountains National Park. This campground is more primitive and remote, so it's less crowded than the other campgrounds in the park. All campsites have a fire ring, picnic table, and several trees. This campground is better suited for tents and small RVs (under 25 feet). The paved pull-in sites are smaller than most, and the road through the campground is small, with some tight turns. A number of hiking trails are easily accessible from Cosby Campground, including the Appalachian Trail, just 3 miles away via the Lower Gap Trail. One trail leads to the Mount Cammerer fire tower, a very popular hiking destination. Fishing in nearby streams is another popular activity.

2 Elkmont

Location: Off Little River Road
GPS coordinates: 35.660549 / -83.583871
Facilities and amenities: Tables, grills, fire rings, tent pads; flush toilets; centrally located water; dump station
Elevation: 2,150 feet
Road conditions: Paved
Hookups: WE
Sites: 220
Maximum RV length: 35 feet
Season: Mar–Nov
Fee: $$$
Maximum stay: 14 days
Management: Great Smoky Mountains National Park; (423) 436-1230; campground inquiries: (865) 430-5560
Reservations: (877) 444-6777; recreation.gov/camping/campgrounds/232487
Pets: Yes
Quiet hours: 10 p.m.–6 a.m.
ADA compliant: Yes
Cell service: None
Activities: Hiking, fishing, swimming, wildlife watching

Relaxing streamside at Elkmont Campground, Great Smoky Mountains National Park

Finding the campground: From Gatlinburg take US 441 2 miles to the Sugarlands Visitor Center and turn right onto Little River Road. Go 4.9 miles and turn left into Elkmont at the sign. Follow this road 1.5 miles to the campground.

About the campground: Elkmont was once a small community before the park bought the land. There are still several reminders of that community, including the old hotel and several vacation cottages, which are no longer used. This is a great campground, very large with three different camping sections. A stream that runs through the campground is used by both fishing enthusiasts and swimmers looking to beat the summer heat. The campground is well maintained, with large sites. The official word is that the campground can handle RVs of 34-foot length, but I saw several that were much larger. Elkmont is a good central location for visiting both the Gatlinburg and Townsend areas.

3 Cades Cove

Location: South end of the park near Townsend
GPS coordinates: 35.660549 / -83.583871
Facilities and amenities: Tables, lantern posts, fire rings, grills; flush toilets; centrally located water; dump station; camp store, riding stables
Elevation: 2,150 feet
Road conditions: Paved
Hookups: WE
Sites: 159
Maximum RV length: 40 feet
Season: Year-round; no reservations taken between Nov 1 and May 14
Fee: $$$
Maximum stay: 14 days
Management: Great Smoky Mountains National Park; (865) 436-1230; campground: (865) 448-4103
Reservations: recreation.gov/camping/campgrounds/232488
Pets: Yes
Quiet hours: 10 p.m.–6 a.m.
ADA compliant: Yes
Cell service: Spotty
Activities: Hiking, bicycling, horseback riding, wildlife watching, auto touring
Finding the campground: From Townsend take US 321 North for 1.2 miles to Little River Road. Turn right onto Laurel Creek Road and go 7.5 miles into Cades Cove; turn left at the sign and go 0.2 mile to the campground.
About the campground: This is one of the more popular camping spots in the park, due in part to the fact that Cades Cove is a very well-known area for wildlife watching. There is also great historical significance in this valley. A one-way, 11-mile loop road travels around the cove and returns near the campground. There are many stops along the way to view old homesteads and rustic cabins. During early morning and late afternoon, you can see white-tailed deer and sometimes black bears in the fields along the road. The campground is a nice one, with plenty of shade and large, level spots. It is very common for wildlife to roam through the campground, so food storage regulations are strictly enforced. A riding stable near the campground provides visitors an opportunity to rent horses and ride the trails around the cove.

Mountain stream in the Smokies

4 Abrams Creek

Location: Near Fontana Lake
GPS coordinates: 35.611602 / -83.932985
Facilities and amenities: Tables, fire rings, grills, lantern posts; flush toilets; centrally located water
Elevation: 1,125 feet
Road conditions: Paved; steep and narrow
Hookups: No
Sites: 16
Maximum RV length: N/A
Season: May–Oct
Fee: $$
Maximum stay: 14 days
Management: Great Smoky Mountains National Park; (865) 436-1230; campground: (865) 448-4103
Reservations: recreation.gov/camping/campgrounds/273847
Pets: Yes
Quiet hours: 10 p.m.–6 a.m.
ADA compliant: Yes
Cell service: None
Activities: Hiking, fishing, wildlife viewing
Finding the campground: From Maryville take US Highway 321 North 10 miles to the Foothills Parkway. Turn right onto the parkway and go west 16.9 miles to where the parkway ends at US 129. Turn left and go 0.1 mile; turn left onto Happy Valley Road and travel 6 miles. Look for the Abrams Creek Campground sign, and turn right onto Abrams Creek Road; follow this road 0.7 mile to the campground. (***Caution:*** The road into the campground is very steep and narrow in places, with room for only one vehicle.)
About the campground: Abrams Creek is very secluded and used mostly by locals and people looking to get away from the crowds. It is a smaller camping area, and the sixteen sites fill quickly on summer weekends. There are hiking trails near the campground. Abrams Creek flows through the campground, providing swimming and fishing opportunities. During summer it's a great place to stay cool because of the large trees that shade the campsites. Abrams Creek is more suited for tent camping; the sites are small, and the road is not big enough for large or even smaller RVs. If you are looking for quiet and solitude, this is the place.

Area 5: Crossville, Oak Ridge, and Wartburg

Oak Ridge is the "Secret City" with a big story to tell. On 60,000 acres of farmland between the Cumberland Plateau and the Great Smoky Mountains, Clinton Engineer Works was one of three secret cities selected by President Franklin Roosevelt for the sole purpose of developing the atomic bomb. What was known then as the Manhattan Project brought 75,000 people to this planned community, but you couldn't find it on any maps in 1943. Once the work was complete, the city opened to the public in 1949 and became known as Oak Ridge. It continues to lead the way in research and development in energy, nuclear research, and medical and materials research.

Crossville is located atop the beautiful Cumberland Plateau and is known as the golf capital of Tennessee, with ten championship golf courses. The rural area offers an abundance of outdoor possibilities, with mountainous wildlife reserves, lakes, streams, and Cumberland Mountain State Park. Just outside Crossville, near Cumberland Mountain State Park, is the community of Homestead. Homestead started in the early and mid-1930s to provide the people of Cumberland County with jobs and low-cost housing. Most of the original houses in this area were made with Crab Orchard stone, which was quarried nearby. The Homestead Tower, located in the center of the community, at one time housed the project's administrative offices. The 85-foot-tall tower was also a water tank that served the surrounding homes. It is now a museum that houses many artifacts from the community's beginnings.

Wartburg was founded in the 1840s by German and Swiss immigrants who named the settlement after Wartburg Castle in Germany. Wartburg was officially incorpo-

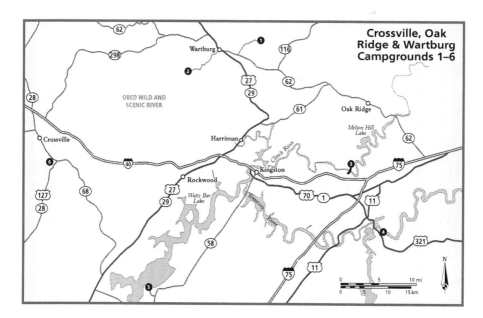

Crossville, Oak Ridge & Wartburg Campgrounds 1–6

Campground number	Campground	Group Sites	RV Sites	Total Sites	Max RV Length	Hookups	Toilets	Showers	Drinking water	Dump station	Pets	ADA Sites	Recreation	Fees ($)	Season	Can reserve	Stay limit (days)
1	Frozen Head State Park	2		28	25 ft		F	•	•		•	•	HWMFR	$–$$$$		•	28
2	Rock Creek			11			V				•	•	HSFPCW	$		•	14
3	Melton Hill Dam		44	61	40 ft	WES	F	•	•	•	•	•	SFBLPW	$$–$$$$		•	21
4	Yarberry		97	97	75 ft	WES	F	•	•	•	•	•	BLPSF	$$$$	Varies	•	Varies
5	Fooshee Pass		52	55	50 ft	WE	F	•		•	•	•	BLPSF	$$–$$$$	Mar–Nov	•	Varies
6	Cumberland Mountain State Park	1	100	145	72 ft	WES	F	•	•	•	•	•	SFBLPWM	$$$$		•	Varies

Hookups: W = Water   E = Electric   S = Sewer

Toilets: F = Flush   V = Vault   C = Chemical

Recreation: H = Hiking   S = Swimming   F = Fishing   B = Boating   L = Boat launch   R = Horseback riding   O = Off-road driving   W = Wildlife watching   M = Mountain biking
C = Rock climbing   G = Golf   P = Paddling

If no entry under Season, campground is open all year. If no entry under Fee, camping is free.

Campground Fee Ranges (per night): $=$10 or less $$=$11–$20 $$$=$21–$30 $$$$=$31 and above

rated in 1851. Today it is best known for its natural beauty and outdoor activities. Just outside of town you'll find Frozen Head State Park, the Obed Wild and Scenic River, Lone Mountain State Forest, Catoosa Wildlife Management Area, the Cumberland Trail, Historic Rugby Tennessee, and the Historic Brushy Mountain Penitentiary.

For more information:
Oak Ridge Chamber of Commerce
1400 Oak Ridge Turnpike
Oak Ridge 37830
(865) 483-1321
oakridgechamber.org

Crossville Chamber of Commerce
34 South Main St.
Crossville 38555
(931) 484-8444
crossvillechamber.com

Morgan County Chamber of Commerce
PO Box 539
Wartburg 37887
(423) 346-5740
morgancountychamber.com

1 Frozen Head State Park

Location: East of Wartburg
GPS coordinates: 36.133278 / -84.498033
Facilities and amenities: Tables, grills, fire rings, lantern posts; flush toilets; centrally located water; playground, horse trails
Elevation: 3,324 feet
Road conditions: Paved
Hookups: None
Sites: 28
Maximum RV length: 25 feet
Season: Year-round
Fee: $-$$$$
Maximum stay: 28 days
Management: Frozen Head State Park; (423) 346-3318
Reservations: reserve.tnstateparks.com/frozen-head/campsites
Pets: Yes
Quiet hours: 10 p.m.–6 a.m.
ADA compliant: Yes
Cell service: Good
Activities: Hiking, fishing, mountain biking, horseback riding
Finding the campground: From US 27 in Wartburg take TN 62 East for 1.9 miles. Turn left onto Flat Fork Road and follow it 3.8 miles to the park entrance; follow signs to the campground.
About the campground: This state park's campground is relatively small compared with other state parks. With only 28 well-spaced-out campsites, camping here is a quiet and relaxing experience. While this campground has no onsite hookups, it does have hot showers. Frozen Head gets its name from 3,324-foot Frozen Head Mountain; the top of this peak is sometimes white from snow or heavy frost while the valley below is not. Not far from the campground you'll find 50 miles of hiking trails, including the Jeep Road Trail. This 6.9-mile trail is used for hiking, mountain biking, and horseback riding. If you want to horseback ride here, you must bring your own horse; there is no place to keep horses overnight. The 11,876 acres that make up this park provide some of the richest wildflower habitat in Tennessee. Peak blooming is approximately mid-April.

2 Rock Creek, Obed Wild and Scenic River

Location: West of Wartburg
GPS coordinates: 36.070559 / -84.664453
Facilities and amenities: Tables, grills, fire rings, lantern posts; vault toilets
Elevation: 990 feet
Road conditions: Paved; dirt in the campground
Hookups: None
Sites: 11
Maximum RV length: N/A
Season: Year-round
Fee: $
Maximum stay: 14 days
Management: Obed Wild and Scenic River, National Park Service; (423) 346-6294
Reservations: recreation.gov/camping/campgrounds/253502?tab=campsites
Pets: Yes
Quiet hours: 10 p.m.–6 a.m.
ADA compliant: Yes
Cell service: Poor
Activities: Kayaking, canoeing, swimming, fishing, hiking, wildlife viewing
Finding the campground: From downtown Wartburg, turn onto Spring Street next to the jail. Spring Street soon becomes Catoosa Road; follow it for 5.8 miles and cross the bridge at the Obed River. Just past the bridge turn right into Rock Creek Campground.

View of the Obed Wild and Scenic River

About the campground: This is a small, primitive campground. Each site is well marked off, with small rustic fences separating the roads from the sites. There is river access right at the campground for kayaks or canoes. Some wonderful hiking trails leave from the campground. The Cumberland Trail, which stretches from Georgia to Kentucky, passes through the campground. There is no drinking water—so bring plenty.

3 Melton Hill Dam

Location: South of Oak Ridge

GPS coordinates: 35.881331 / -84.296873

Facilities and amenities: Tables, lantern posts, grills, tent pads; flush toilets, showers; centrally located water; dump station; beach

Elevation: 820 feet

Road conditions: Paved

Hookups: WES

Sites: 61

Maximum RV length: 40 feet

Season: Year-round

Fee: $$–$$$$

Maximum stay: 21 days

Management: Tennessee Valley Authority; (865) 988-2432

Reservations: camprrm.com/parks/tennessee/tva-6/melton-hill-dam-campground/

Pets: Yes

Quiet hours: 10 p.m.–6 a.m.

ADA compliant: Yes

Cell service: Good

Activities: Boating, fishing, swimming, short nature trail

Finding the campground: From I-40 west of Knoxville, take exit 364 and go north on TN 95 for 0.8 mile. Turn right into the entrance to Melton Hill Dam.

This old bridge over the Obed River is now part of the Cumberland Trail.

About the campground: Melton Hill Dam Campground is a great site for several reasons. For the full-time RVer it's not far from the interstate for an overnight or few days' stay. For someone wishing to camp but still be able to get to the city, it's only a few miles from Oak Ridge, Knoxville, and Lenoir City. This campground is a great place for fishing enthusiasts, with a boat launch and good clean sites on the water.

4 Yarberry

Location: Lenoir City
GPS coordinates: 35.7694 / -84.2177
Facilities and amenities: Tables, grills; showers, flush toilets; dump station; electric, water, and sewer hookups
Elevation: 787 feet
Road conditions: Paved
Hookups: WES
Sites: 97
Maximum RV length: 75 feet
Season: Year-round
Fee: $$$$
Maximum stay: Varies; long-term available
Management: Tennessee Valley Authority; (865) 986-3993
Reservations: reservations.camprrm.com/campground/7/pick_date
Pets: Yes
Quiet hours: 10 p.m.–6 a.m.
ADA compliant: Yes
Cell service: Good
Activities: Swimming, fishing, boating, paddling, water sports
Finding the campground: From Lenoir City, follow US 321 North to Newberry Drive and turn left. Make a slight right onto Yedear Road in 300 feet. Continue 0.2 mile and turn left onto Yarberry Road. Continue for 0.8 mile and turn right to stay on Yarberry Road. The campground will be on the right in 0.1 mile.
About the campground: Yarberry Peninsula Campground offers many amenities and is conveniently located 4 miles from Lenoir City in the foothills of the Great Smoky Mountains. Yarberry is located on the shores of Fort Loudoun Lake, providing stunning views from just about every site. The large, level sites accommodate large RVs and are also great for tents. All sites have 50/30-amp service and water hookups. There are two bathhouses with air and heat for year-round comfort. A picnic table and fire ring is available at each campsite. Yarberry also has a wide range of rental watercraft, from pontoons to paddleboards. The day-use area has a sandy beach as well as picnic tables and grills.

5 Fooshee Pass

Location: Ten Mile
GPS coordinates: 35.6611 / -84.7612
Facilities and amenities: Tables, grills; showers, flush toilets; dump station; electric and water hookups
Elevation: 754 feet
Road conditions: Paved
Hookups: WE
Sites: 55
Maximum RV length: 50 feet
Season: Mar–Nov
Fee: $$–$$$$
Maximum stay: Varies; long-term available
Management: Tennessee Valley Authority; (865) 361-1233
Reservations: reservations.camprrm.com/campground/51/pick_date
Pets: Yes
Quiet hours: 10 p.m.–6 a.m.
ADA compliant: Yes
Cell service: Good
Activities: Swimming, fishing, boating, water sports, paddling
Finding the campground: From I-75, take exit 60. Continue west on TN 68 for 14.5 miles. Turn north on TN 304 and continue 2 miles. Turn left onto Huff Bend Road and continue 1 mile to the recreation area.
About the campground: Fooshee Pass Campground and Recreation Area is located on Watts Bar Lake. It is a great place to camp, hang out, and enjoy the many recreational activities on the lake. Many campers enjoy taking their boat out and skiing, fishing, or just enjoying the lake and the mountains. Many also enjoy canoeing, kayaking, and relaxing in the beach area. The campground has fifty-five sites (fifty-two RV sites, three tent sites), and all sites have water and electric hookups. Each site has a picnic table, grill, and fire ring. There is a boat ramp, playground area, swim area, bathhouse, hot showers, and a dump station.

6 Cumberland Mountain State Park

Location: Crossville

GPS coordinates: 35.900445 / -84.997207

Facilities and amenities: Tables, grills, lantern posts; showers, flush toilets; dump station; electrical and water hookups, 14 sites with sewer hookups; campground store, restaurant, golf course

Elevation: 1,775 feet

Road conditions: Paved

Hookups: WES

Sites: 145

Maximum RV length: 72 feet

Season: Year-round

Fee: $$$$

Maximum stay: 14 nights (Mar 1–Nov 30), 28 nights (Dec 1–Feb 29)

Management: Cumberland Mountain State Park; (800) 250-8618

Reservations: reserve.tnstateparks.com/cumberland-mountain/campsites

Pets: Yes

Quiet hours: 10 p.m.–6 a.m.

ADA compliant: Yes

Cell service: Spotty

Activities: Swimming, fishing, hiking, golf, paddleboats

Finding the campground: From downtown Crossville take US 127 South for 3.6 miles, where US 127 turns right. From here go 0.7 mile and turn right onto TN 419 north. This is also the entrance to the park; the campground is 0.2 mile ahead on the right.

About the campground: Cumberland Mountain State Park began as part of the greater Cumberland Homesteads Project, a New Deal–era initiative by the Resettlement Administration that helped relocate poverty-stricken families on the Cumberland Plateau to small farms centered on what is now the Cumberland Homestead community. This 1,720-acre park was acquired in 1938 to provide a recreational area for some 250 families selected to homestead on the Cumberland Plateau. The park is located around Byrd Lake, a man-made lake created by the impoundment of Byrd Creek in the 1930s. The park provides numerous recreational activities, including hiking, swimming, picnicking and interpretive programs.

Area 6: Cherokee National Forest, Southern Districts

The southern districts of the Cherokee National Forest stretch from the southern tip of Great Smoky Mountains National Park to the Georgia state line and are bordered on the east by North Carolina. This is a vast area of managed forest, scenic drives, mountain peaks, whitewater streams, and recreation areas. The opportunities for recreation are endless. Here you can find the Cherohala Skyway, a 43-mile National Scenic Byway that winds its way over mountain peaks between Tellico Plains, Tennessee, and Robbinsville, North Carolina. Some of the best whitewater rafting and kayaking in the country are located in the Ocoee District. The beautiful Ocoee Whitewater Center was home to the 1996 Summer Olympics whitewater competition. If fishing is more your speed, you'll surely enjoy the Hiwassee and Tellico Rivers; both are popular spots for reeling in large trout. Hiking and mountain biking trails abound in the Tanasi Trail system near the Ocoee Whitewater Center. A few other outdoor activities found in the area include hunting, boating, water-skiing, nature photography, and wildlife viewing. There is something here for just about everyone.

There are several designated camping areas within the Tellico Ranger District, in the Tellico River and North River Corridors. These areas are spread throughout the corridors and are marked with roadside signs. I haven't listed each individual camping area because they are primitive areas where camping is allowed rather than "campgrounds." Some are nothing more than spots in a field, with no marked sites or facilities; others have a portable toilet. Camping here is free because there are no amenities. Be sure to practice Leave No Trace Principles in all situations.

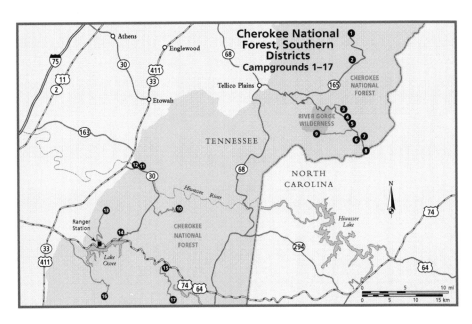

Campground number	Campground	Group Sites	RV Sites	Total Sites	Max RV Length	Hookups	Toilets	Showers	Drinking water	Dump station	Pets	ADA Sites	Recreation	Fees ($)	Season	Can reserve	Stay limit (days)
1	Jake Best			8			V				•		HFWO	$	Mar–Nov		14
2	Indian Boundary		87	87	30 ft	WE	F	•	•	•	•	•	HSFBLPWM	$$	Apr–Nov	•	14
3	North River			11			V				•		HSFW	$			14
4	Dam Creek			10			V				•		HFWO	$			14
5	Spivey Cove			16			V				•		HWO	$			14
6	Davis Branch			6			V				•		HFSWO	$			14
7	Birch Branch			7			V				•		HFWO	$			14
8	State Line			11			V				•		HFWOM	$			14
9	Holly Flatts			15			V				•		HFSWO	$	May–Nov		14
10	Lost Creek			15			V				•	•	HFWO				14
11	Gee Creek	8	30	47	85 ft		F	•	•	•	•	•	HPFWLR	$$–$$$		•	14
12	Lost Corral Horse Camp			20	40 ft		V		•		•	•	RHPFW	$$		•	14
13	Chillowee	1	29	70	90 ft	WE	F	•	•	•	•	•	HFSWPM	$$	April–Oct	•	14
14	Parksville Lake	24	16	40	50 ft	WE	F	•	•	•	•	•	HFSWPMBL	$$–$$$$		•	14
15	Thunder Rock	1		37	20 ft		F	•	•		•	•	HFSWPM	$$		•	14
16	Sylco			12							•		HWO				14
17	Tumbling Creek			8							•		HWOF				14

Hookups: W = Water   E = Electric   S = Sewer

Toilets: F = Flush   V = Vault   C = Chemical

Recreation: H = Hiking   S = Swimming   F = Fishing   B = Boating   L = Boat launch   R = Horseback riding   O = Off-road driving   W = Wildlife watching

M = Mountain biking   C = Rock climbing   G = Golf   P = Paddling

If no entry under Season, campground is open all year. If no entry under Fee, camping is free.

Campground Fee Ranges (per night): $=$10 or less $$=$11–$20 $$$=$21–$30 $$$$=$31 and above

For more information:
Forest Supervisor Office
2800 North Ocoee St.
PO Box 2010
Cleveland 37320
(423) 476-9700

Tellico-Hiwassee Ranger District
250 Ranger Station Rd.
Tellico Plains 37385
(423) 253-2520

Ocoee-Hiwassee Ranger District
Rte. 1, Box 3480
Benton 37307
(423) 338-5201

1 Jake Best, Cherokee National Forest

Location: Cherokee National Forest, Tellico District
GPS coordinates: 35.445969 / -84.109306
Facilities and amenities: Tables, grills, lantern posts, fire rings; vault toilets
Elevation: 1,049 feet
Road conditions: Gravel, rough with narrow bridges
Hookups: None
Sites: 8
Maximum RV length: N/A
Season: Mar–Nov
Fee: $
Maximum stay: 14 days
Management: Cherokee National Forest, Tellico Ranger District; (423) 253-2520
Reservations: No; first come, first served
Pets: Yes
Quiet hours: 10 p.m.–6 a.m.
ADA compliant: No
Cell service: None
Activities: Fishing, hiking, wildlife viewing, off-roading
Finding the campground: From the junction of TN 68 and TN 165E, take TN 165E 14.3 miles. Turn left onto FR 345 and travel 1.2 miles. Turn right onto gravel FR 35 and continue for 2.3 miles to a fork; stay left and go another 5.2 miles. Jake Best is on the right.
About the campground: Jake Best is a small but very well-kept campground on Citico Creek. Trout fishing is good all up and down Citico Creek. Most people who camp here are anglers or people looking for solitude. The road into the campground is gravel and has some narrow bridges, but smaller RVs can camp here.

2 Indian Boundary

Location: Cherokee National Forest, Tellico District
GPS coordinates: 35.401310 / -84.106028
Facilities and amenities: Tables, grills, fire rings, lantern posts; flush toilets, showers; dump station; camp store, beach, boat launch
Elevation: 1,804 feet
Road conditions: Paved
Hookups: WE
Sites: 87
Maximum RV length: 30 feet
Season: Apr–Nov; limited camping in winter
Fee: $$
Maximum stay: 14 days
Management: Cherokee National Forest, Tellico Ranger District; (423) 253-2520; campground inquiries: (423) 253-8400
Reservations: (877) 444-6777; recreation.gov/camping/campgrounds/232215
Pets: Yes
Quiet hours: 10 p.m.–6 a.m.
ADA compliant: Yes
Cell service: Poor
Activities: Fishing, paddling, boating, swimming, hiking, mountain biking
Finding the campground: From the junction of TN 68 and TN 165E, take TN 165E for 14.3 miles. Turn left onto FR 345 and continue 1.2 miles to the entrance to Indian Boundary Recreation Area.
About the campground: This is a beautiful facility. The campground has three large loops; sites on each loop vary from basic to sites with electric hookups. The 96-acre lake has some great fishing. Bass, bluegill, catfish, and trout can all be caught. Only nonmotorized boats or boats with electric motors are allowed on the lake, which makes for a peaceful paddling or fishing experience. There is a wheelchair-accessible fishing pier near Loop A. A 3-mile trail loops around the lake and can be used for either hiking or bicycles. The lake also has a swimming beach for summertime fun. Winter camping is allowed in the overflow area, but there are no hookups or showers here.

3 North River

Location: Cherokee National Forest, Tellico District
GPS coordinates: 35.318395 / -84.125345
Facilities and amenities: Tables, grills, fire rings, lantern posts; vault toilets
Elevation: 1,870 feet
Road conditions: Paved and gravel
Hookups: None
Sites: 11
Maximum RV length: N/A
Season: Year-round
Fee: $
Maximum stay: 14 days
Management: Cherokee National Forest, Tellico Ranger District; (423) 252-2520
Reservations: No; first come, first served
Pets: Yes
Quiet hours: 10 p.m.–6 a.m.
ADA compliant: No
Cell service: None
Activities: Fishing, swimming, hiking, off-road driving, gravel biking
Finding the campground: From the junction of TN 68 and TN 165E, take TN 165E. Go 5.2 miles and turn right onto FR 210; continue 9.7 miles and turn left onto FR 217. Go 2.7 miles; the campground is on the right. Most of FR 217 is gravel, but it's smooth and wide.
About the campground: This is one of the more popular small campgrounds in Cherokee National Forest. The sites here are level, smooth, and very large. Like most of the other campgrounds here, this one is next to a stream that is used for swimming and fishing at the campground.

4 Dam Creek

Location: Cherokee National Forest, Tellico District
GPS coordinates: 35.312420 / -84.120699
Facilities and amenities: Tables, grills; vault toilets; picnic pavilion
Elevation: 1,837 feet
Road conditions: Gravel
Hookups: None
Sites: 10
Maximum RV length: N/A
Season: Year-round
Fee: $
Maximum stay: 14 days
Management: Cherokee National Forest, Tellico Ranger District; (423) 253-2520
Reservations: No; walk-in only; first come, first served
Pets: Yes
Quiet hours: 10 p.m.–6 a.m.
ADA compliant: No
Cell service: Poor
Activities: Fishing, hiking, off-roading
Finding the campground: From the junction of TN 68 and TN 165E, take TN 165E and go 5.2 miles. Turn right onto FR 210 and continue 12.2 miles. Turn left into the parking area.
About the campground: Dam Creek is a dual-purpose area—a day-use picnic area and a walk-in-only campground. The campground is primitive; only picnic tables and bear-proof food lockers designate each site. Walking into the area, you first notice the beautiful stonework and the log pavilion that were constructed by the Civilian Conservation Corps in 1930.

5 Spivey Cove

Location: Cherokee National Forest, Tellico District

GPS coordinates: 35.303824 / -84.113146

Facilities and amenities: Tables, grills, fire rings, lantern posts; vault toilets. The water pump located here is not in use; water must be obtained at North River Campground.

Elevation: 1,935 feet

Road conditions: Paved and gravel

Hookups: None

Sites: 16

Maximum RV length: N/A

Season: Year-round

Fee: $

Maximum stay: 14 days

Management: Cherokee National Forest, Tellico Ranger District; (423) 253-2520

Reservations: No; first come, first served

Pets: Yes

Quiet hours: 10 p.m.–6 a.m.

ADA compliant: No

Cell service: Poor

Activities: Fishing, hiking; nearby swimming, off-roading

Finding the campground: From the junction of TN 68 and TN 165E, take TN 165E and go 5.2 miles. Turn right onto FR 210; continue 12.8 miles and turn left into the entrance. The road through the campground is gravel and is not recommended for large RVs.

About the campground: Spivey Cove is near FR 210 but far enough off the main road so that you feel more in the wilderness. The sites vary in size but aren't suitable for large RVs. A couple of sites share a pull-in parking spot, which would be good for a group that wanted to camp together. The gravel road is traveled only by folks camping here and is a good place for kids to ride their bikes. The campground is very shaded and quiet.

6 Davis Branch

Location: Cherokee National Forest, Tellico District
GPS coordinates: 35.278977 / -84.096548
Facilities and amenities: Tables, grills, fire rings, lantern posts; vault toilets
Elevation: 2,263 feet
Road conditions: Paved
Hookups: None
Sites: 6
Maximum RV length: N/A
Season: Year-round
Fee: $
Maximum stay: 14 days
Management: Cherokee National Forest, Tellico Ranger District; (423) 253-2520
Reservations: No; first come, first served
Pets: Yes
Quiet hours: 10 p.m.–6 a.m.
ADA compliant: No
Cell service: None
Activities: Fishing, hiking, swimming; nearby off-roading
Finding the campground: From the junction of TN 68 and TN 165E, take TN 165E and go 5.2 miles. Turn right onto FR 210 and continue 15.7 miles. The campground is on the left between the road and Tellico River.
About the campground: With only six sites, Davis Branch is very limited on space. The camping area is well maintained and clean, but it is basically right on the side of the main road, with the sites only about 20 yards from the road. The sites here are very large and could accommodate a 36-foot RV.

7 Birch Branch

Location: Cherokee National Forest, Tellico District
GPS coordinates: 35.281649 / -84.098565
Facilities and amenities: Tables, grills, fire rings, lantern posts; vault toilets
Elevation: 2,132 feet
Road conditions: Paved
Hookups: None
Sites: 7
Maximum RV length: N/A
Season: Year-round
Fee: $
Maximum stay: 14 days
Management: Cherokee National Forest, Tellico Ranger District; (423) 253-2520
Reservations: No reservation required; first come, first served
Pets: Yes
Quiet hours: 10 p.m.–6 a.m.
ADA compliant: No
Cell service: None
Activities: Fishing, hiking, swimming; nearby off-road driving
Finding the campground: From Tellico Plains, turn onto TN 165 and go approximately 5 miles. Turn right onto FR 210, going past the ranger station. The campground is approximately 15 miles upstream.
About the campground: Not far from Davis Branch, this is one of several small campgrounds on Tellico River Road (FR 210). This campground offers seven campsites with spacious tent platforms, a picnic table, fire ring, and lantern post. It's located right next to the Tellico River, making it ideal for campers who want to start fishing at the crack of dawn.

8 State Line

Location: Cherokee National Forest, Tellico District
GPS coordinates: 35.261664 / -84.080976
Facilities and amenities: Tables, grills, fire rings, lantern posts; centrally located water; vault toilets
Elevation: 2,591 feet
Road conditions: Paved
Hookups: None
Sites: 11
Maximum RV length: N/A
Season: Year-round
Fee: $
Maximum stay: 14 days
Management: Cherokee National Forest, Tellico Ranger District; (423) 253-2520
Reservations: No; first come, first served
Pets: Yes
Quiet hours: 10 p.m.–6 a.m.
ADA compliant: No
Cell service: None
Activities: Fishing, hiking, mountain biking, off-roading
Finding the campground: From the junction of TN 68 and TN 165E, take TN 165E and go 5.2 miles. Turn right onto FR 210 and continue 17.8 miles. The campground is at the end of the road.
About the campground: The big draw at this campground is the off-roading possibilities. Just past the campground are the North Carolina state line and some of the best four-wheel-drive roads and trails in the Southeast. This area is well known in the off-road circuit, and this campground serves as a base for off-road enthusiasts. The sites are large and can accommodate midsize RVs, but there are no hookups.

⑨ Holly Flatts

Location: Cherokee National Forest, Tellico District
GPS coordinates: 35.285658 / -84.178734
Facilities and amenities: Tables, grills, fire rings; vault toilets
Elevation: 1,870 feet
Road conditions: Gravel, narrow and winding
Hookups: None
Sites: 15
Maximum RV length: N/A
Season: May–Nov
Fee: $
Maximum stay: 14 days
Management: Cherokee National Forest, Tellico Ranger District; (423) 253-2520
Reservations: No; first come, first served
Pets: Yes
Quiet hours: 10 p.m.–6 a.m.
ADA compliant: No
Cell service: None
Activities: Fishing, hiking, swimming, off-roading, wildlife watching
Finding the campground: From the junction of TN 68 and TN 165E, take TN 165E and go 5.2 miles. Turn right onto FR 210 and continue for 13.9 miles. Turn right onto FR 126; go 5.9 miles and turn left into the campground. FR 126 is gravel and has some potholes, but a passenger car can easily make this drive. Some sections of the road are narrow with sharp curves, so pulling a camper trailer on this road is not recommended.

About the campground: Holly Flats is located along the banks of Bald River in a remote location within the Cherokee National Forest. The campground is quiet and secluded, with excellent fishing and hiking opportunities nearby. There are fifteen campsites, and each rustic site has a picnic table, camping pad, grill, and lantern post.

10 Lost Creek

Location: Cherokee National Forest, Ocoee/Hiwassee District

GPS coordinates: 35.159869 / -84.467991

Facilities and amenities: Tables, fire rings, grills; centrally located water; vault toilets

Elevation: 1,089 feet

Road conditions: Gravel

Hookups: None

Sites: 15

Maximum RV length: N/A

Season: Year-round

Fee: None

Maximum stay: 14 days

Management: Cherokee National Forest, Ocoee/Hiwassee Ranger District; (423) 338-5201

Reservations: No; first come, first served

Pets: Yes

Quiet hours: 10 p.m.–6 a.m.

ADA compliant: Yes

Cell service: Poor

Activities: Hiking, fishing, wildlife viewing, off-roading

Finding the campground: From US 64, turn onto TN 30 and go 6 miles. Turn right on FR 103; it's 7 miles to the campground.

About the campground: Lost Creek is another secluded camping area in the Cherokee National Forest located on the banks of Big Lost Creek, which has some good trout fishing. (**Note:** Special regulations are in effect for fishing in Big Lost Creek.) Creature comforts are limited here, but the campground is clean and orderly, offering camping for tents and small pull-behind campers. This is a good place to stay if you enjoy hiking, as the campground is located near the Benton MacKaye Trail.

11 Gee Creek

Location: Cherokee National Forest, Ocoee/Hiwassee Scenic River State Park
GPS coordinates: 35.233115 / -84.547123
Facilities and amenities: Tables, grills, fire rings, lantern posts; flush toilets, showers; centrally located water; boat launch, playground, hiking path, educational programs
Elevation: 721 feet
Road conditions: Paved
Hookups: None
Sites: 47
Maximum RV length: 85 feet
Season: Year-round
Fee: $$–$$$
Maximum stay: 14 days
Management: Hiwassee/Ocoee Scenic River State Park; (423) 263-0050
Reservations: tnstateparks.com/parks/campground/hiwassee-ocoee
Pets: Yes
Quiet hours: 10 p.m.–6 a.m.
ADA compliant: Yes
Cell service: Good
Activities: Hiking, paddling, tubing, fishing, horseback riding
Finding the campground: From Benton, head north on US 411 for 7 miles. Turn right onto Spring Creek Road. The campground is 0.8 mile on the right.
About the campground: Hiwassee State Scenic Rivers' Gee Creek campground is a haven and a home-away-from-home to many river users. Campsites are primitive, tent-friendly, and some sites are close enough to the river that you can be lulled to sleep by the sound of rushing water. A nature trail circles the campground and follows along the river's edge. The park offers year-round

Gee Creek Falls

programming and is a great base camp for fishing, hiking, and paddling. The campground is listed as primitive, with no hookups, and use of generators is not allowed. Tent camping is permitted along most of the John Muir Trail above the Appalachia Powerhouse. It is a USDA Forest Service-managed area of the Cherokee National Forest.

12 Lost Corral Horse Camp

Location: Cherokee National Forest, Ocoee/Hiwassee Scenic River State Park
GPS coordinates: 35.237608 / -84.547814
Facilities and amenities: Tables, grills, fire rings, lantern posts, horse hitching post; centrally located water; vault toilets
Elevation: 721 feet
Road conditions: Paved to gravel
Hookups: None
Sites: 20
Maximum RV length: 40 feet
Season: Year-round
Fee: $$
Maximum stay: 14 days
Management: Hiwassee/Ocoee Scenic River State Park; (423) 263-0050
Reservations: fs.usda.gov/recarea/cherokee/recarea/?recid=35120
Pets: Yes
Quiet hours: 10 p.m.–6 a.m.
ADA compliant: Yes
Cell service: Spotty
Activities: Horseback riding, hiking, paddling, tubing, fishing
Finding the campground: From the US 64/US 411 intersection go north on US 411 approximately 12 miles; turn right at the Gee Creek Campground sign. Go approximately 1 mile, turn left just past the state park office, and cross the railroad tracks; the campground is to the left.
About the campground: Located at the entrance to the Starr Mountain and Chestnut Mountain Horse Trails, this campground features twenty roomy campsites, each with a picnic table, fire ring, lantern post, and horse hitching area (high line). The sites accommodate up to five people and two vehicles. There is a public water supply and vault toilet facilities.

13 Chilhowee

Location: Cherokee National Forest, Ocoee/Hiwassee District
GPS coordinates: 35.152164 / -84.608661
Facilities and amenities: Tables, grills, fire rings, lantern posts; flush toilets, showers; centrally located water; dump station; electric hookups; beach
Elevation: 1,968 feet
Road conditions: Paved, steep
Hookups: WE
Sites: 70
Maximum RV length: 90 feet
Season: Apr–Oct
Fee: $$
Maximum stay: 14 days
Management: Cherokee National Forest, Ocoee/Hiwassee Ranger District; (423) 338-5201
Reservations: recreation.gov/camping/campgrounds/251723
Pets: Yes
Quiet hours: 10 p.m.–6 a.m.
ADA compliant: Yes
Cell service: Spotty
Activities: Hiking, mountain biking, swimming, fishing
Finding the campground: From the Ocoee Ranger Station, take FR 77, which begins next to the entrance to the ranger station. Go 7.3 miles to the campground sign; turn right and continue 0.5 mile to the campground. Follow the signs.
About the campground: Located in the Chilhowee Recreation Area, Chilhowee Campground offers more than seventy campsites, electric hookups, RV sites, tent-only sites, and multiple bathhouses. The campground is open from early April to late October, with an overflow area and day-use area open year-round. The 7-acre McKamy Lake offers a swim area with a sand beach and fishing from the bank. Boats are allowed, but gasoline motors are not. Also within the recreation area are approximately 25 miles of hiking and biking trails and scenic Benton Falls. On the drive up to the campground, stop at one of the many observation overlooks to view beautiful mountain settings. Wildlife is abundant in this area, so tread lightly and have your camera ready.

Benton Falls

14 Parksville Lake

Location: Cherokee National Forest, Ocoee/Hiwassee District
GPS coordinates: 35.116938 / -84.575217
Facilities and amenities: Tables, grills, fire rings, lantern posts; showers, flush toilets; centrally located water; dump station; electric hookups
Elevation: 853 feet
Road conditions: Paved
Hookups: WE
Sites: 40
Maximum RV length: 50 feet
Season: Year-round
Fee: $$–$$$$
Maximum stay: 14 days
Management: Cherokee National Forest, Ocoee/Hiwassee Ranger District; (423) 338-5201; campground: (423) 338-3300
Reservations: recreation.gov/camping/campgrounds/251438
Pets: Yes
Quiet hours: 10 p.m.–6 a.m.
ADA compliant: Yes
Cell service: Spotty
Activities: Fishing, swimming, boating, canoeing, kayaking, hiking, mountain biking—all nearby

Swimming beach on Parksville Lake

The view of Parksville Lake from Chilhowee Mountain

Finding the campground: From the Ocoee Ranger Station, take US 64 East for 2.2 miles. Turn left onto TN 30; the campground is 0.2 mile ahead. Group camping is on the right side of the road; RV camping is on the left.

About the campground: Parksville Lake Campground offers well-shaded and nicely spaced campsites that can accommodate larger RVs. The campground is divided into two sections. One side of the road is for group camping without any hookups. The other side of TN 30 is for family camping, up to five people per campsite, and has electric hookups. Not far from the campground are mountain biking trails that lead up to the Chilhowee Campground. A half mile away on US 64 is Parksville Lake. Parksville Lake is the oldest lake in the Cherokee National Forest, created by the Tennessee Rural Electric Company in 1910–11. Sometimes known as Lake Ocoee, it is now controlled by the Tennessee Valley Authority (TVA). Scenic views of the 1,930-acre lake can be found along the Ocoee Scenic Byway. The lake is popular for motorboating. There are two public boat launches and a marina located along US 64. You can also swim and picnic at Mac Point or Parksville Beach on US 64. Just below the dam is Sugarloaf Park, where visitors can picnic, view a scale model of the Olympic canoe and kayak course, or set off on a paddling or tubing adventure down the lower Ocoee River.

15 Thunder Rock

Location: Cherokee National Forest, Ocoee/Hiwassee District
GPS coordinates: 35.076148 / -84.485133
Facilities and amenities: Tables, grills, fire rings, lantern posts; flush toilets, showers; centrally located water
Elevation: 1,299 feet
Road conditions: Paved
Hookups: None
Sites: 37
Maximum RV length: 20 feet
Season: Year-round
Fee: $$
Maximum stay: 14 days
Management: Cherokee National Forest, Ocoee/Hiwassee District; (423) 338-5201
Reservations: recreation.gov/camping/campgrounds/251938
Pets: Yes
Quiet hours: 10 p.m.–6 a.m.
ADA compliant: Yes
Cell service: Poor
Activities: Whitewater kayaking, canoeing, rafting, swimming, hiking, mountain biking
Finding the campground: From the Ocoee Ranger Station take US 64 East for 10.8 miles. Turn right at the sign for Ocoee Powerhouse Number 3. Cross the bridge and drive around the powerhouse; the campground is on the other side.
About the campground: Thunder Rock is the nearest campground to the site of the 1996 Olympic whitewater venue. The Whitewater Center is 0.6 mile east on US 64. The center holds several events throughout the year, including many naturalist events, making this campground popular among whitewater and outdoor enthusiasts. The campground itself is located next to the Ocoee River. When water is being diverted to produce electricity at the powerhouse, the pools of water left in the river are great for swimming. Even though there are no hookups here, several sites are big enough to accommodate larger RVs.

16 Sylco

Location: Cherokee National Forest, Ocoee/Hiwassee District
GPS coordinates: 35.026614 / -84.601295
Facilities and amenities: Tables, grills
Elevation: 1,155 feet
Road conditions: Gravel, rough and narrow
Hookups: None
Sites: 12
Maximum RV length: N/A
Season: Year-round
Fee: None
Maximum stay: 14 days
Management: Cherokee National Forest, Ocoee/Hiwassee Ranger District; (423) 338-5201
Reservations: No; first come, first served
Pets: Yes
Quiet hours: 10 p.m.–6 a.m.
ADA compliant: No
Cell service: None
Activities: Primitive camping, fishing, gravel biking, off-roading
Finding the campground: From the Ocoee Ranger Station take US 64 West for approximately 3 miles to Cookson Creek Road. Turn left onto Cookson Creek Road, which becomes FR 55; follow the signs 10 miles to the campground.
About the campground: This is a primitive campground with no facilities, including no water. Sylco is a long way from most other recreation areas in Cherokee National Forest; keep this in mind when planning a camping trip here.

17 Tumbling Creek

Location: Cherokee National Forest, Ocoee/Hiwassee District
GPS coordinates: 35.017382 / -84.467301
Facilities and amenities: Tables, grills, lantern posts
Elevation: 4,000 feet
Road conditions: Gravel, rough and narrow
Hookups: None
Sites: 8
Maximum RV length: N/A
Season: Year-round
Fee: None
Maximum stay: 14 days
Management: Cherokee National Forest, Ocoee/Hiwassee Ranger District; (423) 338-5201
Reservations: No; first come, first served
Pets: Yes
Quiet hours: 10 p.m.–6 a.m.
ADA compliant: No
Cell service: None
Activities: Primitive camping, fishing, hiking, off-roading
Finding the campground: From the Ocoee Ranger Station, take US 64 East for 10.8 miles. Turn right at the sign for Ocoee Powerhouse 3. Cross the bridge and take FR 45 for 2 miles to FR 221. Turn left onto FR 221 and travel 6 miles to the campground.
About the campground: Tumbling Creek and Sylco are not much different, although there seems to be more to do in the Tumbling Creek area. Camping is primitive, with no water or restroom, and the road into the campground is not very wide. It took about 30 minutes each way to reach the campground. It is far enough out to get that wilderness feeling.

Area 7: Chattanooga

Surrounded by mountains and a river that runs through the heart of downtown, Chattanooga has earned a reputation as a premier outdoor destination. Located in southeast Tennessee in the foothills of the Appalachian Mountains, Chattanooga was once known as the dirtiest city in America, but over the past forty years, has worked to clean up its act and reinvent itself. The revitalized downtown district features the world's largest freshwater aquarium, the iconic Walnut Street Bridge, the Tennessee Riverwalk, and a variety of shops, eateries, breweries, museums, theaters, and art galleries. Within an hour's drive from the bustle of the revitalized and vibrant downtown districts, you'll find world-class rock climbing, mountain biking, paddling, hiking, and more. It's easy to see why Chattanooga was voted "Best Town Ever" twice by *Outside* magazine readers. Today Chattanooga is a vacation destination, and tourism has a major impact on the economy.

Fun facts: Chattanooga is home to the world's largest freshwater aquarium, the first place Coca-Cola was bottled, the birthplace of miniature golf, home to the steepest passenger incline railway in the country, and where the tow truck was invented.

For more information:
Outdoor Chattanooga
200 River St.
Chattanooga 37405
(423) 643-6888
outdoorchattanooga.com

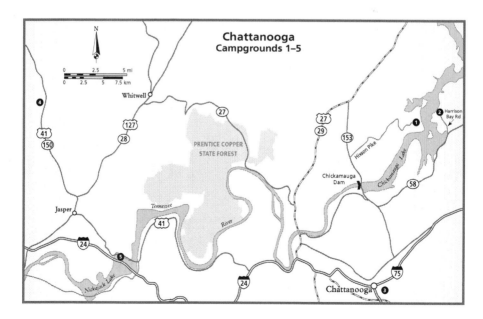

Campground number	Campground	Group Sites	RV Sites	Total Sites	Max RV Length	Hookups	Toilets	Showers	Drinking water	Dump station	Pets	ADA Sites	Recreation	Fees ($)	Season	Can reserve	Stay limit (days)
1	Chester Frost Park		190	225	77 ft	WE	F	•	•	•	•	•	•	HSFBLPW	$$–$$$		•	14–28
2	Harrison Bay State Park	1	128	149	65 ft	WE	F	•	•	•	•	•	•	HSFBLPWMG	$$$–$$$$		•	14–28
3	Camp Jordan		58	58	70 ft	WE	F	•	•	•	•	•	•	HFPWLB	$$		•	14
4	Foster Falls		25	25	34 ft		F	•	•		•	•	•	HCW	$$		•	14
5	Marion County Park	1	20	29	65 ft	WE	F	•	•	•	•	•		SFBLP	$$			14

Hookups: W = Water   E = Electric   S = Sewer

Toilets: F = Flush   V = Vault   C = Chemical

Recreation: H = Hiking   S = Swimming   F = Fishing   B = Boating   L = Boat launch   R = Horseback riding   O = Off-road
    driving   W = Wildlife watching   M = Mountain biking   C = Rock climbing   G = Golf   P = Paddling

If no entry under Season, campground is open all year. If no entry under Fee, camping is free.

Campground Fee Ranges (per night): $=$10 or less $$=$11–$20 $$$=$21–$30 $$$$=$31 and above

1 Chester Frost Park

Location: Chickamauga Lake, near Chattanooga
GPS coordinates: 35.182971 / -85.142042
Facilities and amenities: Tables, grills, lantern posts; shower, flush toilets; laundry; centrally located water; dump station; water and electric hookups; playground, boat launch, beach, disc golf course, sand volleyball court
Elevation: 688 feet
Road conditions: Paved
Hookups: WE
Sites: 225
Maximum RV length: 77 feet
Season: Year-round; not all sites open winter months
Fee: $$-$$$
Maximum stay: 14–28 days
Management: Hamilton County Parks and Recreation; (423) 842-1077; campground: (423) 209-6894
Reservations: hamilton.itinio.com/chester-frost/camping
Pets: Yes
Quiet hours: 10 p.m.–6 a.m.
ADA compliant: Yes
Cell service: Good
Activities: Boating, paddling, water-skiing, swimming, fishing, bicycling, horseback riding
Finding the campground: From TN 153 at NorthGate Mall, go north on TN 319, also known as Hixson Pike. Take Hixson Pike 4.1 miles and watch for the sign to Chester Frost Park. Turn right onto Gold Point Road and go 2.2 miles to the park and campground entrance.
About the campground: This huge park and campground is just outside the Chattanooga metropolitan area. From the campground it's about a 20-minute drive to the downtown area. The campground itself is on sort of an island, surrounded by water and accessed by a narrow strip of land. The camping area is well divided, with tent sites in one area and RV sites in another. There are lakefront sites for both tents and RVs; if being on the lake is not your thing, there are sites on the hills overlooking the lake. This is a popular summer spot for boats, personal watercraft, and fishing enthusiasts; boats can be anchored at the lakeside campsites. There are two boat ramps and several fishing piers. There's also a disc golf course, playground, sand volleyball court, and swim beach area.

A group of paddlers at sunset at Chester Frost

2 Harrison Bay State Park

Location: Chickamauga Lake, near Chattanooga
GPS coordinates: 35.170809 / -85.124309
Facilities and amenities: Tables, grills, fire rings, lantern posts; showers, flush toilets; dump station; electrical and water hookups; camp store, marina, restaurant, boat rentals, boat launch
Elevation: 650 feet
Road conditions: Paved
Hookups: WE
Sites: 149
Maximum RV length: 65 feet
Season: Year-round
Fee: $$$–$$$$
Maximum stay: 14–28 days
Management: Harrison Bay State Park; (423) 344-6214
Reservations: reserve.tnstateparks.com/harrison-bay/campsites
Pets: Yes
Quiet hours: 10 p.m.–6 a.m.
ADA compliant: Yes
Cell service: Good
Activities: Water sports, boating, paddling, fishing, swimming beach, hiking, mountain biking, golf
Finding the campground: From TN 153 and TN 58, take TN 58 North for 8 miles. Turn left onto Harrison Bay Road and go 1.5 miles; turn left into the state park entrance.
About the campground: Harrison Bay State Park is due east across Chickamauga Lake from Chester Frost and is basically the same type of camping area. One of the big pluses to camping here is the marina and restaurant. The campground also has a swimming beach. Being located so close to Chattanooga, Harrison Bay fills up early on summer weekends, but it isn't all that crowded on weekdays. The sites on the water fill up first. Most sites are shady and have plenty of room. There is a 4.5-mile loop trail for hiking and biking.

3 Camp Jordan

Location: East Ridge
GPS coordinates: 34.999322 / -85.200303
Facilities and amenities: Bathhouse, pavilion; centrally located water; water and electric hook-ups; canoe/kayak launch
Elevation: 679 feet
Road conditions: Paved to gravel
Hookups: WE
Sites: 58
Maximum RV length: 70 feet
Season: Year-round
Fee: $$
Maximum stay: 14 days
Management: City of East Ridge; (423) 490-0078
Reservations: eastridgeparksandrec.com/page/show/5808285-rv-campground
Pets: Yes
Quiet hours: 10 p.m.–6 a.m.
ADA compliant: Yes
Cell service: Good
Activities: Hiking, biking, paddling, fishing, disc golf
Finding the campground: From downtown Chattanooga take I-24 East toward East Ridge. Take the I-75 South split toward Atlanta. Take exit 1 for I-75 South. Turn left off the exit and left again on to Camp Jordan Parkway.
About the campground: This multiuse facility has a variety of recreational activities, including a paved walking path, a pond to fish in, a kayak/canoe launch onto Chickamauga Creek, disc golf, a playground, and several ball fields. Short-term overnight camping is permitted in a gravel lot that offers water and electric hookups.

4 Foster Falls

Location: North of Jasper
GPS coordinates: 35.182503 / -85.671581
Facilities and amenities: Tables, grills, fire rings, lantern posts; showers, flush toilets; centrally located water
Elevation: 1,739 feet
Road conditions: Paved
Hookups: None
Sites: 25
Maximum RV length: 34 feet
Season: Year-round
Fee: $$
Maximum stay: 14 days
Management: South Cumberland State Park; (931) 924-2980
Reservations: reserve.tnstateparks.com/south-cumberland/campsites
Pets: Yes
Quiet hours: 10 p.m.–6 a.m.
ADA compliant: Yes
Cell service: Good
Activities: Hiking, rock climbing
Finding the campground: From downtown Jasper take US 41 North for 8.7 miles. Turn left at the sign for Foster Falls Campground and continue 0.4 mile to the entrance.

Foster Falls, the waterfall for which the campground is named

About the campground: This is a popular weekend spot among the active crowd, with hiking and rock climbing popular activities. The campground is named for a beautiful waterfall that is within walking distance. The campground is a beautiful facility that is well taken care of by both campers and the folks who manage it. The camping fee is set by the unit; a tent or an RV is a unit, and more than one of either can be on a site.

5 Marion County Park

Location: Southwest of Chattanooga
GPS coordinates: 35.031842 / -85.560234
Facilities and amenities: Concrete tables; showers, restroom; fishing pier; water and electric hookups
Elevation: 623 feet
Road conditions: Paved
Hookups: WE
Sites: 29
Maximum RV length: 65 feet
Season: Year-round
Fee: $$
Maximum stay: 14 days
Management: Marion County Parks; (423) 942-6653
Reservations: (423) 942-6653
Pets: Yes
Quiet hours: 10 p.m.–6 a.m.
ADA compliant: Yes
Cell service: Good
Activities: Fishing, swimming, boating, paddling
Finding the campground: From the junction of I-24 West and TN 156, take TN 156 East for 0.9 mile to its intersection with US 41 North. Take US 41 North for 1.2 miles and turn left into the campground entrance.
About the campground: Its location not far from I-24 makes this campground a likely spot for passing travelers. Surrounded by water, this campground has a fishing pier and boat launch. There's a small, unimproved beach area for swimming. The campground has marked sites for RVs, but tent camping is mostly open, and several tents can be placed together. There are showers and restroom facilities.

Area 1: Cookeville, Cordell Hull Lake, Dale Hollow Lake

Nestled among the hills of the Cumberland Plateau, Cookeville is a charming college town and outdoor oasis boasting 150 waterfalls within an hour's drive. Home to Tennessee Tech University, Cookeville is conveniently located near I-40 between Nashville (79 miles west) and Knoxville (101 miles east), and 100 miles north of Chattanooga on TN 111. Both Cordell Hull and Dale Hollow Lakes are located within an hour's drive of Cookeville and provide 1,200 miles of shoreline.

Many of the campgrounds in Middle Tennessee are US Army Corps of Engineers properties, including Cordell Hull and Dale Hollow. Dale Hollow, in the upper corner of this area near the Tennessee–Kentucky state line, is renowned for its fishing opportunities. In addition to yielding the world-record smallmouth bass and being known as a trophy smallmouth lake, the Obey River below Dale Hollow Dam is also known for excellent rainbow and brown trout fishing. Cordell Hull Lake is slightly west of Cookeville; it's a smaller reservoir than Dale Hollow but with equally beautiful scenery and good fishing.

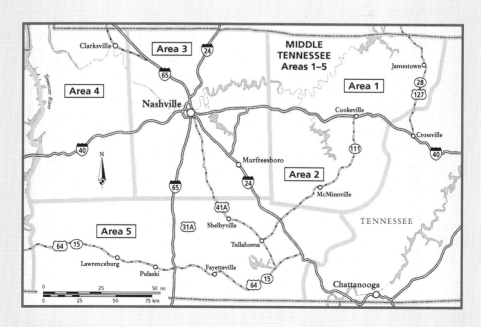

For more information:
Cookeville-Putnam County Visitors Bureau
113 West Broad St., Ste. A
Cookeville 38501
(931) 526-2211
visitcookevilletn.com

Cookeville Chamber of Commerce
1 West 1st St.
Cookeville 38501
(931) 526-2211; (800) 264-5541
cookevillechamber.com

Cordell Hull fishing information:
(615) 735-1050
Dale Hollow fishing information:
(931) 243-3408

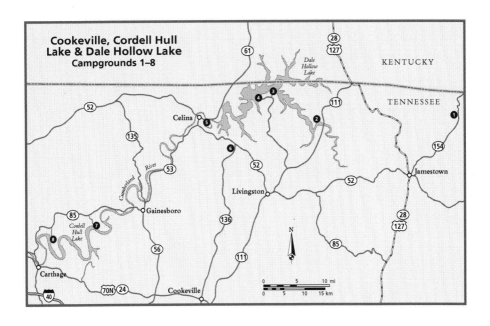

Campground number	Campground	Group Sites	RV Sites	Total Sites	Max RV Length	Hookups	Toilets	Showers	Drinking water	Dump station	Pets	ADA Sites	Recreation	Fees ($)	Season	Can reserve	Stay limit (days)
1	Pickett CCC Memorial State Park		26	26	34 ft	WE	F	•	•	•	•	•	HSW	$$-$$$		•	14
2	Obey River	4	99	127	90 ft	WE	F	•	•	•	•	•	FSWBL	$$$-$$$$	Apr-Oct	•	14
3	Lillydale	1	84	113	70 ft	WE	F	•	•	•	•	•	FSWBLH	$$$-$$$$	Apr-Sept	•	14
4	Willow Grove	1	61	82	75 ft	WE	F	•	•	•	•	•	FSWBLH	$$$-$$$$	May-Sept	•	14
5	Dale Hollow Dam	3	71	72	75 ft	WE	F	•	•	•	•	•	FSWBLH	$$$$	Apr-Oct	•	14
6	Standing Stone State Park		36	36	45 ft	WE	F	•	•	•	•	•	HFPW	$$$-$$$$		•	14
7	Salt Lick Creek	1	150	150	110 ft	WES	F	•	•	•	•	•	BLPFWH	$$-$$$	Apr-Oct	•	14
8	Defeated Creek		124	155	80 ft	WES	F	•	•	•	•	•	BLPFWH	$$$-$$$$	Mar-Nov	•	14

Hookups: W = Water   E = Electric   S = Sewer

Toilets: F = Flush   V = Vault   C = Chemical

Recreation: H = Hiking   S = Swimming

F = Fishing   B = Boating   L = Boat launch   R = Horseback riding   O = Off-road driving   W = Wildlife watching   M = Mountain biking   C = Rock climbing   G = Golf
P = Paddling

If no entry under Fee, camping is free.

Campground Fee Ranges (per night): $ = $10 or less $$ = $11-$20 $$$ = $21-$30 $$$$ = $31 and above

1 Pickett CCC Memorial State Park

Location: North of Jamestown
GPS coordinates: 36.551056 / -84.796639
Facilities and amenities: Grills, tables; flush toilets, showers; dump station; water and electric hookups; swimming pool
Elevation: 1,542 feet
Road conditions: Paved
Hookups: WE
Sites: 26
Maximum RV length: 34 feet
Season: Year-round
Fee: $$–$$$
Maximum stay: 14 days
Management: Pickett CCC Memorial State Park; (931) 879-5821
Reservations: reserve.tnstateparks.com/pickett/campsites
Pets: Yes
Quiet hours: 10 p.m.–6 a.m.
ADA compliant: Yes
Cell service: Spotty
Activities: Hiking, swimming, rowboats
Finding the campground: From Jamestown, take TN 154 North for 15 miles. The entrance to the state park and campground is on the left.

Ranger Station, Pickett State Park

The Natural Bridge at Pickett State Park

About the campground: Located within the 19,200-acre Pickett State Forest, Pickett Civilian Conservation Corps Memorial State Park is best known for its geological features. The park contains numerous bridges and caves and is adjacent to the 125,000-acre Big South Fork National River and Recreation Area, making it an ideal base camp for exploring the variety of hiking trails at either Pickett or Big South Fork. The sites here are smaller and suited more to tents, pop-up campers, and small pull-behind trailers. The park also offers several cabin rentals.

2 Obey River

Location: Dale Hollow Lake, east of Celina
GPS coordinates: 36.531586 / -85.168150
Facilities and amenities: Tables, grills; flush toilets, showers; laundry; dump station; water and electric hookups; boat launch, playground
Elevation: 656 feet
Road conditions: Paved
Hookups: WE
Sites: 127
Maximum RV length: 90 feet
Season: Apr–Oct
Fee: $$$–$$$$
Maximum stay: 14 days
Management: US Army Corps of Engineers; (931) 864-6388
Reservations: (931) 243-3136; Recreation.gov
Pets: Yes
Quiet hours: 10 p.m.–6 a.m.
ADA compliant: Yes
Cell service: Good
Activities: Fishing, boating, water-skiing, swimming
Finding the campground: From the junction of TN 52 and TN 111, take TN 111 North for 1.5 miles; TN 111 turns left. Continue on TN 111 for 13 miles; the entrance to the campground is on the left.
About the campground: Obey is a large campground on the shore of Dale Hollow Lake. Its location near TN 111 makes this a very accessible campground. A commercial marina and restaurant are located near the entrance to Obey Campground, so this is not a wilderness experience. But it is a great location for boating, fishing, and family fun. This is a good, clean campground with plenty of large, level sites. Laundry and showers are available on-site.

3 Lillydale

Location: Dale Hollow Lake
GPS coordinates: 36.604506 / -85.301440
Facilities and amenities: Tables, grills, lantern poles, fire rings; flush toilets, showers; laundry; dump station; water and electric hookups; boat launch, beach
Elevation: 688 feet
Road conditions: Paved
Hookups: WE
Sites: 113
Maximum RV length: 70 feet
Season: Apr–Sept
Fee: $$$–$$$$
Maximum stay: 14 days
Management: US Army Corps of Engineers; (931) 823-4155
Reservations: recreation.gov/camping/campgrounds/232623
Pets: Yes
Quiet hours: 10 p.m.–6 a.m.
ADA compliant: Yes
Cell service: Good
Activities: Fishing, boating, water-skiing, hiking, volleyball, swimming beach
Finding the campground: From the junction of TN 52W and TN 111N/294 in Livingston, take TN 111N/294 North for 1.7 miles. TN 111N/294 turns left; go 3.7 miles, where TN 294 turns left. From here TN 294 is also known as Willow Grove Road. Follow Willow Grove Road for 13.8 miles. Turn right onto Lillydale Road and continue 0.9 mile to the campground.
About the campground: The campground is surrounded by a dense canopy of forest, and a hiking trail snakes through the landscape and along the lakeshore. Lillydale has the most lakefront campsites on Dale Hollow Lake, including a walk-in, tent-only section located on a small island. The Accordion Bluff Hiking Trail is a 7.5-mile one-way trail that ascends to a ridgetop and back down to the shoreline of Dale Hollow Lake. The trail is ideal for birders and wildflower enthusiasts. This trail connects both Lillydale and Willow Grove Campgrounds and can be accessed via the trailhead located at the campground. The campground offers two boat ramps and two swimming beaches.

4 Willow Grove

Location: Dale Hollow Lake
GPS coordinates: 36.587176 / -85.342763
Facilities and amenities: Tables, grills, lantern poles, fire rings; flush toilets, showers; laundry; dump station; water and electric hookups; boat launch, beach
Elevation: 656 feet
Road conditions: Paved
Hookups: WE
Sites: 82
Maximum RV length: 75 feet
Season: May–Sept
Fee: $$$–$$$$
Maximum stay: 14 days
Management: US Army Corps of Engineers; (931) 823-4285
Reservations: recreation.gov/camping/campgrounds/232747
Pets: Yes
Quiet hours: 10 p.m.–6 a.m.
ADA compliant: Yes
Cell service: Good
Activities: Fishing, boating, water-skiing, beach, swimming, volleyball, hiking
Finding the campground: From the junction of TN 52W and TN 111N/294 in Livingston, take TN 111N/294 North for 1.7 miles. TN 111N/294 turns left; go 3.7 miles, where TN 294 turns left. From here TN 294 is also known as Willow Grove Road. Follow Willow Grove Road for 16 miles to the campground entrance.
About the campground: Willow Grove is a beautiful campground, with sites that vary from hilltop spots overlooking Dale Hollow Lake to sites that are closer to the water. Some sites are in the open; others are shaded by large hardwood trees. A 7.5-mile hiking trail, the Accordion Bluff Nature Trail, connects Willow Grove and Lillydale Campgrounds.

5 Dale Hollow Dam

Location: Dale Hollow Lake
GPS coordinates: 36.538451 / -85.460013
Facilities and amenities: Tables, fire rings, grills, lantern poles; flush toilets, showers; laundry; dump station; water and electric hookups; fish-cleaning stations
Elevation: 641 feet
Road conditions: Paved
Hookups: WE
Sites: 72
Maximum RV length: 75 feet
Season: Apr–Oct
Fee: $$$$
Maximum stay: 14 days
Management: US Army Corps of Engineers; (931) 243-3554
Reservations: recreation.gov/camping/campgrounds/232564
Pets: Yes
Quiet hours: 10 p.m.–6 a.m.
ADA compliant: Yes
Cell service: Some
Activities: Fishing, boat launch, paddling, volleyball

Trout fishing near the campground at Dale Hollow Dam

Finding the campground: From the junction of TN 52W and TN 53N in Celina, take TN 53N north for 3.7 miles. Turn right onto Dale Hollow Dam Road and go 0.4 mile. Turn right onto Campground Road; it's another 0.2 mile to the campground.

About the campground: This is one of the Corps of Engineers' most popular campgrounds for several reasons. The campground is extremely clean and well kept, with excellent restrooms and shower facilities. The area is peaceful. But trout fishing and the Dale Hollow National Fish Hatchery, which sits adjacent to the campground, are the main draw for this campground. Operated by the US Fish and Wildlife Service, the hatchery is the largest federal trout hatchery east of the Mississippi, producing 1.5 million trout annually and helping stock the Obey River. The hatchery is open to visitors daily. The campground is located on the Obey River below Dale Hollow Dam. The temperature of the stream water is a constant 45°F to 47°F, making it great for trout, which are stocked every Friday. There are two fish-cleaning stations with stainless steel sinks and running water—a great setup for cleaning your catch. Nearby is a boat launch ramp.

6 Standing Stone State Park

Location: Northwest of Livingston
GPS coordinates: 36.471418 / -85.415110
Facilities and amenities: Tables, fire rings, lantern poles, grills; flush toilets, showers; dump station; water and electric hookups; swimming pool
Elevation: 885 feet
Road conditions: Paved
Hookups: WE
Sites: 36
Maximum RV length: 45 feet
Season: Year-round
Fee: $$$–$$$$
Maximum stay: 14 days
Management: Standing Stone State Park; (931) 823-6347 or (800) 713-5157
Reservations: tnstateparks.com/parks/campground/standing-stone
Pets: Yes
Quiet hours: 10 p.m.–6 a.m.
ADA compliant: Yes
Cell service: Good
Activities: Hiking, paddling, fishing, wildlife viewing
Finding the campground: From the junction of TN 111 and TN 52 in Livingston, take TN 52 North for 8.6 miles. Turn left onto TN 136 South; go 1.2 miles to the campground entrance, on the left.
About the campground: Standing Stone Sate Park is located in Standing Stone State Forest on the Cumberland Plateau. The park's name comes from a 12-foot-tall rock standing upright on a

Standing Stone State Park

sandstone ledge. This state park campground is smaller than most other state park campgrounds, making for a more peaceful camping experience. The campsites are shaded by large hardwood trees and have plenty of room for RVs (up to 45-foot) or tents. Kelly Lake is a small lake situated within the park that offers fishing as well as canoe, kayak, and rowboat rentals. This park is not far from Dale Hollow Lake.

7 Salt Lick Creek

Location: Cordell Hull Lake

GPS coordinates: 36.320759 / -85.788586

Facilities and amenities: Tables, fire rings, grills, lantern poles; flush toilets, showers; dump station; laundry; water, electric, and some sewer hookups; playground

Elevation: 519 feet

Road conditions: Paved

Hookups: WES

Sites: 150

Maximum RV length: 110 feet

Season: Apr–Oct

Fee: $$–$$$

Maximum stay: 14 days

Management: US Army Corps of Engineers; (931) 638-4718

Reservations: recreation.gov/camping/campgrounds/232697

Pets: Yes

Quiet hours: 10 p.m.–6 a.m.

ADA compliant: Yes

Cell service: None

Activities: Fishing, boating, paddling, water-skiing, beach, swimming

Finding the campground: From downtown Gainesboro, take East Hull Avenue 0.7 mile and turn right onto TN 262 and TN 85 West. Go 9.4 miles and turn left onto Smith Bend Road. Go 1 mile and make a right turn onto Salt Lick Park Lane; continue 0.8 mile to the campground.

About the campground: This is a beautiful campground with lots of sites shaded by hardwood trees and large grassy areas between sites that are very well manicured. The sites near the water gently slope to the water's edge but are very level nonetheless. The sites that are not on the water have the feel of being in the woods. With an on-site visitor center and variety of recreational opportunities, including fishing, paddling, boating, hiking, and biking, this campground is ideal for families and outdoor enthusiasts.

8 Defeated Creek

Location: Cordell Hull Lake
GPS coordinates: 36.302078 / -85.909223
Facilities and amenities: Tables, grills, fire rings, lantern poles; flush toilets, showers; dump station; laundry; water, electric, and some sewer hookups; playground
Elevation: 492 feet
Road conditions: Paved
Hookups: WES
Sites: 155
Maximum RV length: 80 feet
Season: Mar–Nov
Fee: $$$–$$$$
Maximum stay: 14 days
Management: US Army Corps of Engineers; (615) 774-3141
Reservations: recreation.gov/camping/campgrounds/232572
Pets: Yes
Quiet hours: 10 p.m.–6 a.m.
ADA compliant: Yes
Cell service: Some
Activities: Fishing, boating, water-skiing, beach, swimming
Finding the campground: From the intersection of TN 25 and TN 263 in Carthage, take TN 263 North for 5.1 miles. Turn right onto TN 85 East; go 2 miles and turn right onto Marina Lane. Continue 1.4 miles to the campground entrance.
About the campground: Defeated Creek is another great Corps of Engineers campground. This is a good spot for fishing, boating, or just relaxing with friends and family. Sixty-three of the sites have sewer hookups, and all have water and electricity. The sites are large, with plenty of shade, and a commercial marina and restaurant are just outside the campground. A secure parking area is provided for boat trailers, which creates extra room at the sites.

Area 2: Center Hill Lake, McMinnville, and Smithville

Covering 18,200 acres, Center Hill Lake is the largest of the US Army Corps of Engineers lakes in Tennessee. It's also one of the most popular recreation destinations in Middle Tennessee—with good reason. Hiking, fishing, swimming, boating, and many other water sports are enjoyed on Center Hill's beautiful water.

Not far south of Center Hill Lake is the town of McMinnville, with Rock Island and Fall Creek Falls State Parks both nearby. McMinnville, the largest town in this area of Tennessee, is known as "The Nursery Capital of the World." McMinnville and surrounding Warren County are home to over 400 thriving nurseries. Climate and soil conditions combine to offer a near-perfect growing environment. Because McMinnville is a great spot for growing plants, a great time to visit is in spring and early summer, when the flowers are in bloom.

Located closer to Center Hill Lake is the small town of Smithville, home to the world-famous Fiddler's Jamboree, an Appalachian music and craft festival held the first weekend in July since 1972. The small town of around 5,000 persons grows to around 80,000 during the festival, which draws hundreds of musicians and craft vendors along with thousands of spectators from all over the world.

For more information:
McMinnville Chamber of Commerce
110 South Court Square
McMinnville 37110
(931) 473-6611
warrentn.com

Smithville-Dekalb County Chamber of Commerce
712 South Congress Blvd.
Smithville 37166
(615) 597-4163
dekalbtn.org

Fishing Information Hot Line
(931) 858-4366; (615) 548-8581

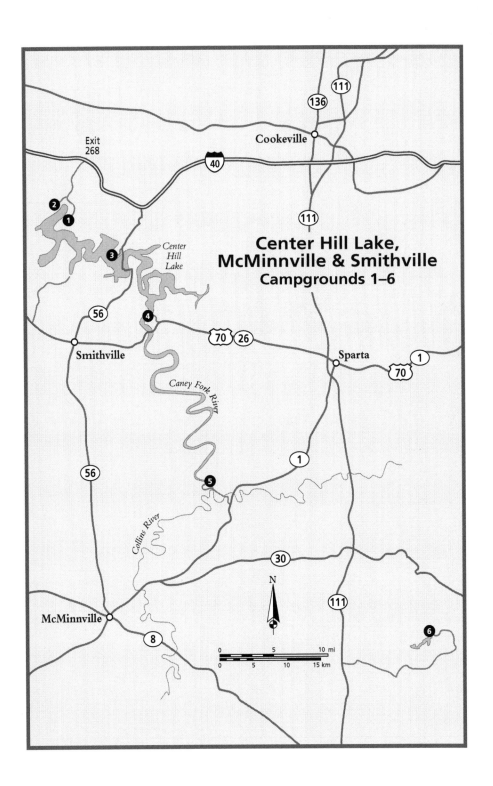

Center Hill Lake, McMinnville & Smithville
Campgrounds 1–6

Campground number	Campground	Group Sites	RV Sites	Total Sites	Max RV Length	Hookups	Toilets	Showers	Drinking water	Dump station	Pets	ADA Sites	Recreation	Fees ($)	Season	Can reserve	Stay limit (days)
1	Edgar Evins State Park		60	60	40 ft	WE	F	•	•	•	•	•	SBLFHP	$$-$$$$	Mar-Oct	•	14
2	Long Branch		60	60	96 ft	WE	F	•	•	•	•	•	FC	$$$	Apr-Oct	•	14
3	Floating Mill Park		115	115	40 ft	WES	F	•	•	•	•	•	FBLHSP	$$$	Apr-Oct	•	14
4	Ragland Bottom		40	56	80 ft	WES	F	•	•	•	•	•	LFBHSP	$$-$$$	Apr-Oct	•	14
5	Rock Island State Park		50	60	55 ft	WE	F	•	•	•	•	•	HFSBLP	$$$-$$$$		•	14
6	Fall Creek Falls State Park	1	92	222	65 ft	WES	F	•	•	•	•	•	HFBSMR	$-$$$$		•	14

Hookups: W = Water   E = Electric   S = Sewer

Toilets: F = Flush   V = Vault   C = Chemical

Recreation: H = Hiking   S = Swimming   F = Fishing   B = Boating   L = Boat launch   R = Horseback riding   O = Off-road driving   W = Wildlife watching   M = Mountain biking   C = Rock climbing   G = Golf   P = Paddling

If no entry under Season, campground is open all year. If no entry under Fee, camping is free.

Campground Fee Ranges (per night): $=$10 or less $$=$11-$20 $$$=$21-$30 $$$$=$31 and above

1 Edgar Evins State Park

Location: Center Hill Lake
GPS coordinates: 36.081126 / -85.832174
Facilities and amenities: Tables, grills, fire rings; flush toilets, showers; laundry; dump station; water and electric hookups; playground; nearby commercial marina and store with boat ramp and water access
Elevation: 754 feet
Road conditions: Paved, steep and winding
Hookups: WE
Sites: 60
Maximum RV length: 40 feet
Season: Mar–Oct; some sites open year-round
Fee: $$-$$$$
Maximum stay: 14 days
Management: Edgar Evins State Park; (931) 858-2446
Reservations: reserve.tnstateparks.com/edgar-evins/campsites. Mar–Oct, call the camp store at (931) 858-2618; Nov–Feb, call the park office at (931) 646-3080.
Pets: Yes
Quiet hours: 10 p.m.–6 a.m.
ADA compliant: Yes
Cell service: Good
Activities: Hiking, fishing, swimming, boating, water-skiing

Relaxing on one of the camping platforms at Edgar Evins State Park

Burgess Falls

Finding the campground: From I-40 west of Cookeville, take exit 268 to TN 96. Go south 3.6 miles to TN 141. The entrance to Edgar Evins State Park is directly across TN 141.

About the campground: Edgar Evins State Park campground sits on the shoreline overlooking Center Hill Lake in the steep, hilly Eastern Highland Rim. The 6,000-acre park provides many recreational opportunities, cabins, and campsites on one of the most beautiful reservoirs in Tennessee. The park also has a large on-site marina with a restaurant and gift shop. All sixty sites here are on platforms that resemble a patio deck. The platforms are built on a hillside using concrete pillars and steel I-beams to create a strong structure that is then covered with wood. The strength is apparent when large RVs are parked on them. It is a great use of a hillside; when it rains, the water drains off quickly so there is never any mud—and all sites are level.

2 Long Branch

Location: Center Hill Lake
GPS coordinates: 36.099108 / -85.831971
Facilities and amenities: Tables, grills, fire rings, lantern poles; flush toilets, showers; laundry; dump station; water and electric hookups
Elevation: 492 feet
Road conditions: Paved
Hookups: WE
Sites: 60
Maximum RV length: 96 feet
Season: Apr–Oct
Fee: $$$
Maximum stay: 14 days
Management: US Army Corps of Engineers; (615) 548-8002
Reservations: (877) 833-6777; recreation.gov/camping/campgrounds/232630/campsites
Pets: Yes
Quiet hours: 10 p.m.–6 a.m.
ADA compliant: Yes
Cell service: Good
Activities: Fishing, paddling, boating, hiking at Edgar Evins State Park
Finding the campground: From I-40 west of Cookeville, take exit 268 to TN 96. Continue for 5 miles to the end of Center Hill Dam. Turn right on TN 141 and follow signs to the campground.
About the campground: Long Branch is located next to Caney Fork River, just below Center Hill Dam. This campground is a mixture of shady and open sites, but all are level and have wooden tables for cleaning fish. The trout fishing here seems to be fairly good and is one of the campground draws. The area is also a good spot to base a canoeing or kayaking trip on the Caney River. About 0.5 mile away is a public boat launch on Center Hill Lake.

3 Floating Mill Park

Location: Center Hill Lake
GPS coordinates: 36.0449 / -85.7634
Facilities and amenities: Tables, grills, fire rings; flush toilets, showers; dump station; laundry; water and electric hookups
Elevation: 656 feet
Road conditions: Paved
Hookups: WES
Sites: 115
Maximum RV length: 40 feet
Season: Apr–Oct
Fee: $$$
Maximum stay: 14 days
Management: US Army Corps of Engineers; (615) 858-4845; (931) 858-4845
Reservations: (877) 444-6777; recreation.gov/camping/campgrounds/232589
Pets: Yes
Quiet hours: 10 p.m.–6 a.m.
ADA compliant: Yes
Cell service: Spotty
Activities: Fishing, boating, water-skiing, swimming, paddling, hiking
Finding the campground: From the junction of TN 56 and US 70 in Smithville, take TN 56 North for 9.6 miles. Turn left onto Floating Mills Road and go 0.7 mile to the three forks in the road; take the middle fork and follow this to the campground.
About the campground: Floating Mill Park is located on the shores of the scenic Center Hill Lake on central Tennessee's Highland Rim. The lake stretches 64 miles up the Caney Fork River, where visitors come to enjoy boating, fishing, and water sports. The 415 miles of forested shoreline provide excellent hiking, hunting, and camping opportunities. This large campground provides a wide variety of campsites, most of which have electric and water hookups, plus several tent-only sites. A day-use group picnic area is available for reservations. Amenities like flush toilets, showers, and drinking water are provided, creating a comfortable camping experience for guests. A boat ramp, fish cleaning station, playground, and hiking trail are all conveniently located within the campground. The campground also has a nice beach area for swimming and a short hiking trail that connects to a day-use area.

4 Ragland Bottom

Location: Center Hill Lake
GPS coordinates: 35.977 / -85.7213
Facilities and amenities: Tables, grills, fire rings, lantern poles; flush toilets, showers; laundry; dump station; water, electric, and some sewer hookups; playground, swimming beach
Elevation: 688 feet
Road conditions: Paved
Hookups: WES
Sites: 56
Maximum RV length: 80 feet
Season: Apr–Oct
Fee: $$–$$$
Maximum stay: 14 days
Management: US Army Corps of Engineers; (615) 761-3616
Reservations: (877) 444-6777; recreation.gov/camping/campgrounds/232684
Pets: Yes
Quiet hours: 10 p.m.–6 a.m.
ADA compliant: Yes
Cell service: Spotty
Activities: Swimming, fishing, boating, water-skiing, paddling, basketball, volleyball, hiking
Finding the campground: From the junction of US 70 and TN 56 in Smithville, take US 70 East for 7.1 miles. Turn left onto Ragland Bottom Road; continue 1.4 miles to the campground entrance.
About the campground: Ragland Bottom Campground is located on the shores of Center Hill Lake on central Tennessee's Highland Rim. The lake stretches 64 miles up the Caney Fork River, where visitors come to enjoy boating, fishing, and water sports. This waterfront campground offers forty sites with water and electric hookups, as well as sixteen primitive tent sites. A large group day-use picnic area is available as well, with water and 15-amp electric hookups. Amenities like flush toilets, showers, and drinking water are provided, creating a comfortable camping experience for guests. A boat ramp, volleyball court, basketball hoop, playground, and hiking trail are all conveniently located within the campground. The adjacent day-use area has a group picnic shelter, boat ramp, and swimming beach.

5 Rock Island State Park

Location: Northeast of McMinnville
GPS coordinates: 35.8122 / -85.6457
Facilities and amenities: Tables, grills, fire rings; flush toilets, showers; dump station; water and electric hookups; playground
Elevation: 885 feet
Road conditions: Paved
Hookups: WE
Sites: 60
Maximum RV length: 55 feet
Season: Year-round for main campground; Mar–Oct for tent sites
Fee: $$$–$$$$
Maximum stay: 14 days
Management: Rock Island State Park; (931) 686-2471
Reservations: reserve.tnstateparks.com/rock-island/campsites
Pets: Yes
Quiet hours: 10 p.m.–6 a.m.
ADA compliant: Yes
Cell service: Good
Activities: Hiking, fishing, swimming beach, boating, paddling

Waterfalls at Rock Island State Park

Finding the campground: From the junction of US 70 and TN 56 in McMinnville, take US 70 East for 12 miles. Turn left onto TN 136 North; go 1.2 miles and turn left onto TN 287 South. Continue 2.2 miles and turn right into the park entrance; follow signs to the campground.

About the campground: Rock Island has two campgrounds. The main campground has fifty sites to accommodate RVs and trailers and is open year-round. The tent-only campground has ten sites, each with 20-amp electrical service, water hookups, fire ring, charcoal grill, and picnic table and is closed November 2 to March 15. Rock Island State Park is an 883-acre park located on the headwaters of Center Hill Lake at the confluence of the Caney Fork, Collins, and Rocky Rivers. The rugged beauty of the park includes the Caney Fork Gorge below Great Falls Dam. These overlooks are some of the most scenic and significant along the Eastern Highland Rim. Great Falls is a 30-foot cascading horseshoe waterfall, located below the nineteenth-century cotton textile mill that it powered more than one hundred years ago. Rock Island became a Tennessee state park in 1969.

6 Fall Creek Falls State Park

Location: South of Cookeville
GPS coordinates: 35.6558 / -85.3525
Facilities and amenities: Tables, grills, fire rings, lantern poles; flush toilets, showers; laundry; dump station; water, electric, and some sewer hookups; camp store, golf course, lodge
Elevation: 1,706 feet
Road conditions: Paved
Hookups: WES
Sites: 222
Maximum RV length: 65 feet
Season: Year-round
Fee: $-$$$$
Maximum stay: 14 days
Management: Fall Creek Falls State Park
Reservations: (423) 881-5298 or (800) 250-8611; reserve.tnstateparks.com/fall-creek-falls/campsites
Pets: Yes
Quiet hours: 10 p.m.–6 a.m.
ADA compliant: Yes
Cell service: Good

Fall Creek Falls

Activities: Hiking, boating, biking, horseback riding, golf, swimming

Finding the campground: From the junction of US 70 and TN 111 in Sparta, go south on TN 111 approximately 22 miles. Turn left onto TN 284 and follow the large brown signs into the park.

About the campground: Fall Creek Falls is one of Tennessee's largest and most visited state parks. The 29,800-acre park is located on the eastern top of the rugged Cumberland Plateau. At 256 feet, the waterfall that bears the park's name is one of the highest free-flowing waterfalls in the eastern United States. Other waterfalls within the park include Piney Falls, Cane Creek Falls, and Cane Creek Cascades. Fall Creek Falls features 30 cabins, 222 campsites in five different areas, an 85-room lodge, and group camping. Backcountry camping is also available with a permit.

Area 3: Nashville

Nashville, the state capital of Tennessee, is best known as the country music capital of the world. But while most people do associate country music and Nashville, there is so much more to Nashville than that. Galleries, museums, historical sites, the Grand Ole Opry, hockey, football, baseball, zoos, and gardens all add to the diversity of this metropolitan area. Several of the campgrounds in this section are just a few miles outside Nashville, making them a good base for a vacation to the Music City. The rest of the campgrounds listed are within an hour's drive of downtown.

For more information:
Nashville Convention & Visitors Corp
(800) 657-6910
visitmusiccity.com

J. Percy Priest Lake information:
(615) 883-2351
percy-priest-lake.com

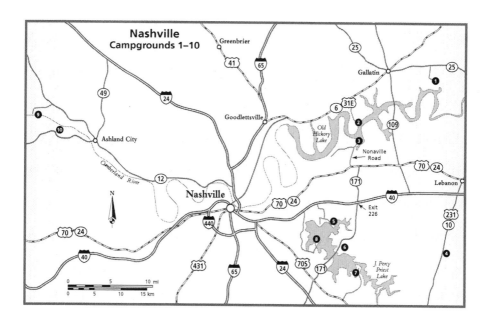

Campground number	Campground	Group Sites	RV Sites	Total Sites	Max RV Length	Hookups	Toilets	Showers	Drinking water	Dump station	Pets	ADA Sites	Recreation	Fees ($)	Season	Can reserve	Stay limit (days)
1	Bledsoe Creek State Park		58	61	65 ft	WE	F	•	•	•	•	•	HFBLP	$$-$$$$		•	14
2	Cages Bend		43	43	50 ft	WE	F	•	•	•	•	•	BFSLP	$$$-$$$$	Apr–Oct	•	14
3	Cedar Creek		60	60	75 ft	WE	F	•	•	•	•		BFSLP	$$$-$$$$	Apr–Oct	•	14
4	Cedars of Lebanon State Park		117	117	60 ft	WE	F	•	•	•	•	•	SRMH	$$$-$$$$		•	14
5	Seven Points		50	60	45 ft	WE	F	•	•	•			BSFLP	$$$-$$$$	Apr–Oct	•	14
6	Long Hunter State Park	2		2					•	•	•		BFSHLC	$-$$		•	14
7	Poole Knobs	1	80	88	40 ft	WE	F	•	•	•	•	•	BPR	$$$-$$$$	May–Sept	•	14
8	Anderson Road		37	37	140 ft	E	F	•	•	•	•	•	HFSBLP	$$$-$$$$	May–Sept	•	14
9	Lock A Recreation Area		38	45	40 ft	WE	F	•	•	•	•	•	HSFBLP	$$$	Apr–Oct	•	14
10	Harpeth River Bridge		15	15	50 ft	WE	F	•	•	•	•	•	FLP	$$$	Apr–Oct	•	14

Hookups: W = Water   E = Electric   S = Sewer

Toilets: F = Flush   V = Vault   C = Chemical

Recreation: H = Hiking   S = Swimming   F = Fishing   B = Boating   L = Boat launch   R = Horseback riding   O = Off-road driving   W = Wildlife watching   M = Mountain biking   C = Rock climbing   G = Golf   P = Paddling

If no entry under Season, campground is open all year. If no entry under Fee, camping is free.

Campground Fee Ranges (per night): $=$10 or less $$=$11–$20 $$$=$21–$30 $$$$=$31 and above

1 Bledsoe Creek State Park

Location: East of Gallatin
GPS coordinates: 36.3785 / -86.3605
Facilities and amenities: Tables, grills; flush toilets, showers; dump station; electric and water hookups; boat launch
Elevation: 426 feet
Road conditions: Paved
Hookups: WE
Sites: 61
Maximum RV length: 65 feet
Season: Year-round
Fee: $$–$$$$
Maximum stay: 14 days
Management: Bledsoe Creek State Park; (615) 452-3706
Reservations: reserve.tnstateparks.com/bledsoe-creek/campsites
Pets: Yes
Quiet hours: 10 p.m.–6 a.m.
ADA compliant: Yes
Cell service: Good
Activities: Hiking, boating, paddling, fishing
Finding the campground: From Gallatin travel east on TN 25 approximately 4.5 miles and turn right onto Zieglers Fort Road. Continue 1.3 miles; the park entrance is on the left.
About the campground: Bledsoe Creek State Park is rich in history. It was once a prime hunting ground for the Cherokee, Creek, Shawnee, and Chickamauga Native American tribes. Once English settlers arrived to the area, the great herds of animals dispersed and never returned. The Bledsoe Creek territory became a Tennessee state park in 1973. The park features 6 miles of scenic hiking trails that meander through the forest and along the lakeshore, and paddling and fishing opportunities on the lake. One mile of trail is paved, making it accessible to persons with disabilities. Bledsoe Creek has fifty-eight paved campsites with fire rings, grills, and picnic tables. All have water hookups. Forty-four campsites can accommodate rigs over 20 feet long; fourteen sites are appropriate for rigs under 20 feet; and three campsites are dedicated for hammock camping. There are two bathhouses with heat and air-conditioning and hot showers.

2 Cages Bend

Location: Old Hickory Lake.
GPS coordinates: 36.3047 / -86.5162
Facilities and amenities: Tables, grills, fire rings, lantern poles; flush toilets, showers; laundry; dump station; electric and water hookups; boat launch, fishing docks; playground and group picnic shelter
Elevation: 459 feet
Road conditions: Paved
Hookups: WE
Sites: 43
Maximum RV length: 50 feet
Season: Apr–Oct
Fee: $$$–$$$$
Maximum stay: 14 days
Management: US Army Corps of Engineers; (615) 824-4989
Reservations: (877) 444-6777; recreation.gov/camping/campgrounds/232539
Pets: Yes
Quiet hours: 10 p.m.–6 a.m.
ADA compliant: Yes
Cell service: Good
Activities: Fishing, boating, water-skiing, paddling, wildlife viewing

Waterfront sites at Cages Bend

Finding the campground: From Gallatin take US 31E south for 5 miles and turn left onto Cages Bend Road. Go 2.9 miles; turn left onto Benders Ferry Road and continue 0.4 mile. The campground is on the left.

About the campground: Cages Bend Campground is located on a grassy knoll on the shores of Old Hickory Lake, offering campers the opportunity to enjoy outdoor activities with a scenic backdrop. Water recreation is the major attraction for lake-goers, but with white-tailed deer, migratory songbirds, and waterfowl in the area, birding and wildlife photography are popular as well. The campground offers a playground for families, a boat ramp for easy lake access, showers for comfort, and a group picnic shelter. All sites have electric and water hookups, with four sites rated as ADA accessible. The campsites are big, and well shaded by the large hardwood trees throughout the campground. Two docks are available for fishing, and there is a boat launch site next to the camping area. Boats can be moored at the lakeside campsites.

3 Cedar Creek

Location: Old Hickory Lake
GPS coordinates: 36.276755 / -86.510772
Facilities and amenities: Tables, grills, fire rings, lantern poles; showers, flush toilets; laundry; dump station; electric and water hookups; boat launch, beach
Elevation: 426 feet
Road conditions: Paved
Hookups: WE
Sites: 60
Maximum RV length: 75 feet
Season: Apr–Oct
Fee: $$$–$$$$
Maximum stay: 14 days
Management: US Army Corps of Engineers; (615) 754-4547
Reservations: (877) 444-6777; recreation.gov/camping/campgrounds/232545
Pets: Yes
Quiet hours: 10 p.m.–6 a.m.
ADA compliant: Yes
Cell service: Good
Activities: Fishing, boating, water-skiing, paddling, swimming
Finding the campground: From Nashville, travel east on I-40 to exit 221A. Continue onto TN 45/ Old Hickory Boulevard. Turn right onto US 70/Lebanon Pike. Turn left onto Nonaville Road and travel until reaching a four-way stop. Turn right at the four-way stop onto Saundersville Road. The recreation area is at the end of the road.
About the campground: Cedar Creek is located on a peninsula on Old Hickory Lake, just 30 minutes from Nashville. The campground is large, level, and well maintained. Most sites are shaded and have ample room between them for privacy. A day-use area next to the campground provides a boat launch and dock.

4 Cedars of Lebanon State Park

Location: South of Lebanon

GPS coordinates: 36.0829 / -86.3214

Facilities and amenities: Tables, grills, fire rings, lantern poles; showers, flush toilets; laundry; dump station; electric and water hookups; swimming pool, playgrounds

Elevation: 623 feet

Road conditions: Paved

Hookups: WE

Sites: 117

Maximum RV length: 60 feet

Season: Year-round; limited camping in winter

Fee: $$$–$$$$

Maximum stay: 14 days

Management: Cedars of Lebanon State Park; (615) 443-2769

Reservations: reserve.tnstateparks.com/cedars-of-lebanon/campsites

Pets: Yes

Quiet hours: 10 p.m.–6 a.m.

ADA compliant: Yes

Cell service: Good

Activities: Swimming, hiking, horseback riding, mountain biking

Finding the campground: From I-40 take the Lebanon exit and go south on US 231 for 6.3 miles. Turn left onto Cedar Forest Road and follow signs; this is also the entrance to the park. Follow this road 0.8 mile to the campground entrance.

The campground: Cedars of Lebanon was named for the dense cedar forest that existed in biblical times, and the reason for this name is apparent everywhere. The 1,139-acre park has 117 campsites in three camping areas equipped with picnic tables, grills, and electric and water hookups.

5 Seven Points

Location: J. Percy Priest Lake
GPS coordinates: 36.1341 / -86.5705
Facilities and amenities: Tables, grills, fire rings, lantern poles; showers, flush toilets; laundry; dump station; electric and water hookups; boat launch, beach
Elevation: 492 feet
Road conditions: Paved
Hookups: WE
Sites: 60
Maximum RV length: 45 feet
Season: Apr–Oct
Fee: $$$–$$$$
Maximum stay: 14 days
Management: US Army Corps of Engineers; (615) 889-5198
Reservations: (877) 444-6777; recreation.gov/camping/campgrounds/232702
Pets: Yes
Quiet hours: 10 p.m.–6 a.m.
ADA compliant: Yes
Cell service: Good
Activities: Fishing, boating, swimming, paddling, water sports
Finding the campground: From downtown Nashville, take I-40 East for 7 miles to exit 221B. Turn right onto Old Hickory Boulevard, then left on Bell Road, right on New Hope Road, and left on Stewarts Ferry Pike. Follow the signs to the campground.
About the campground: Seven Points Campground offers sixty shady and spacious lakeside campsites along with two large picnic shelters on the shores of J. Percy Priest Lake. The campground features drinking water, a dump station, flush toilets, and hot showers, creating a comfortable camping experience. A boat ramp and swimming beach allow guests to take advantage of the vast, sparkling lake. The waterfront sites slope gently to the lake, creating a great place to relax near the water. Boats can be moored at the lakeside sites.

6 Long Hunter State Park

Location: J. Percy Priest Lake.
GPS coordinates: 36.092491 / -86.555832
Facilities and amenities: Picnic tables, fire rings
Elevation: 528 feet
Road conditions: Paved
Hookups: None
Sites: 2 (backcountry-only)
Maximum RV length: N/A
Season: Year-round
Fee: $–$$
Maximum stay: 14 days
Management: Long Hunter State Park; (615) 885-2422
Reservations: reserve.tnstateparks.com/long-hunter/campsites
Pets: Yes
Quiet hours: 10 p.m.–6 a.m.
ADA compliant: Yes
Cell service: Spotty
Activities: Hiking, canoeing, fishing, boating, water sports, swimming
Finding the campground: From I-40, take exit 226 and go south on TN 171 for 6.8 miles. Turn at the sign for the state park.
About the campground: Long Hunter State Park has two backcountry camping sites that are located 6 miles from the parking area. Campers must hike in 6 miles to access either site. One is located right on the shore. Both camping areas are primitive, with no hookups, but they do have picnic tables and fire rings. There are lots of activities for groups to do: hiking, paddling, swimming, and fishing. Reservations must be made in advance, and the fee is based on eight to ten persons maximum capacity at each site.

7 Poole Knobs

Location: J. Percy Priest Lake
GPS coordinates: 36.0545 / -86.5154
Facilities and amenities: Tables, grills, fire rings, lantern poles; showers, flush toilets; laundry; dump station; electric and water hookups; boat launch
Elevation: 557 feet
Road conditions: Paved
Hookups: WE
Sites: 88
Maximum RV length: 40 feet
Season: May–Sept
Fee: $$$–$$$$
Maximum stay: 14 days
Management: US Army Corps of Engineers; (615) 459-6948
Reservations: (877) 444-6777; recreation.gov/camping/campgrounds/232677
Pets: Yes
Quiet hours: 10 p.m.–6 a.m.
ADA compliant: Yes
Cell service: Good
Activities: Fishing, boating, paddling, water sports, horseback riding
Finding the campground: From US 70S (Murfreesboro Pike) in LaVergne, watch for the campground sign and turn onto Fergus Road. Follow Fergus Road 0.8 mile and turn right onto Jones Mill Road. Continue 3.9 miles to the campground.
About the campground: There are two camping areas at Poole Knobs. The first area is near the water, with sites on the lake. Most of the lakeshore is rocky, and there is no beach area. The sites in this section are very nice, with a large camping pad made from timbers and gravel that is perfect for grilling and relaxing. The other section is away from the lake on a forested hilltop. These wooded sites have the look and feel of being much farther from the big city than they really are.

8 Anderson Road

Location: J. Percy Priest Lake
GPS coordinates: 36.1078 / -86.6055
Facilities and amenities: Tables, grills; showers, flush toilets; centrally located drinking water; laundry; dump station; electric hookups; boat launch, beach
Elevation: 492 feet
Road conditions: Paved
Hookups: E
Sites: 37
Maximum RV length: 140 feet
Season: May–Sept
Fee: $$$–$$$$
Maximum stay: 14 days
Management: US Army Corps of Engineers; (615) 361-1980
Reservations: (877) 444-6777; recreation.gov/camping/campgrounds/232515
Pets: Yes
Quiet hours: 10 p.m.–6 a.m.
ADA compliant: Yes
Cell service: Good
Activities: Fishing, boating, swimming, paddling, water sports, hiking
Finding the campground: From downtown Nashville, take I-40 East for 5 miles to exit 219. Turn right on Stewarts Ferry Pike and continue straight on Bell Road for 5 miles. Turn left on Smith Springs Road, then left on Anderson Road. The campground is ahead about 1 mile on the left. Or continue straight on Anderson Road to access the day-use area and shelter.
About the campground: Anderson Road Campground offers thirty-seven shady and spacious campsites. The campground features drinking water, a dump station, a shower house, and a boat ramp. There are no water hookups at the campsite, making it more primitive than other campgrounds in the area. Near the campground is a day-use area with a swimming beach that campers can access with their hangtags. The day-use area also provides picnic tables, grills, a shelter, and a playground. Some sites are waterfront; others are in the cedar trees away from the lake. *Note:* This area may be closed on the weekends due to the high volume of visitors in the area.

⑨ Lock A Recreation Area

Location: Cumberland River–Ashland City
GPS coordinates: 36.317 / -87.1958
Facilities and amenities: Tables, grills, lantern poles; showers, flush toilets; laundry; dump station; electric and water hookups; playground, boat launch
Elevation: 393 feet
Road conditions: Paved
Hookups: WE
Sites: 45
Maximum RV length: 40 feet
Season: Apr–Oct
Fee: $$$
Maximum stay: 14 days
Management: US Army Corps of Engineers; (615) 792-3715
Reservations: (877) 444-6777; recreation.gov/camping/campgrounds/232627
Pets: Yes
Quiet hours: 10 p.m.–6 a.m.
ADA compliant: Yes
Cell service: Good
Activities: Fishing, boating, hiking, paddling
Finding the campground: From Ashland City, take US 12 and go 8 miles west to Cheap Hill. Turn left on Cheatham Dam Road, traveling west 4 miles. Turn left into the campground.
About the campground: Lock A Campground is a wonderful camping area along the banks of the Cumberland River near Cheatham Dam, with large hardwood shade trees adding to the relaxing atmosphere. Large RV sites, plenty of grassy areas, a volleyball court, and a nearby beach make this a great place for the family to camp.

10 Harpeth River Bridge

Location: Harpeth River–Ashland City
GPS coordinates: 36.284 / -87.1453
Facilities and amenities: Tables, grills, fire rings, lantern poles; boat launch; volleyball, playground; flush toilets
Elevation: 360 feet
Road conditions: Paved
Hookups: WE
Sites: 15
Maximum RV length: 50 feet
Season: Apr–Oct
Fee: $$$
Maximum stay: 14 days
Management: US Army Corps of Engineers; (615) 792-4195
Reservations: recreation.gov/camping/campgrounds/251574
Pets: Yes
Quiet hours: 10 p.m.–6 a.m.
ADA compliant: Yes
Cell service: Good
Activities: Paddling, fishing, boat launch
Finding the campground: From Ashland City, head northwest on South Main Street toward Cumberland Street. Take the first left onto TN 49W/Cumberland Street and continue to follow TN 49W for 5 miles. The campground will be on your right, directly before the Harpeth River Bridge.
About the campground: The relaxing, family-friendly atmosphere at Harpeth River Campground is hard to beat. Located on the right bank of the Harpeth River, the water wraps almost all the way around the campground so that every site is a water site. Beautiful old trees provide cool shade on even the hottest days. The campground is located about 10 miles northwest of Ashland City and is a 30-minute drive to Nashville.

Area 4: Land Between the Lakes National Recreation Area

Land Between the Lakes (LBL) is a 170,000-acre national recreation area approximately 90 miles north of Nashville. It is the largest inland peninsula in the United States, stretching into both Tennessee and Kentucky. Formed when the Tennessee and Cumberland Rivers were impounded, creating Kentucky Lake and Lake Barkley, LBL was designated a national recreation area in 1963 by President John F. Kennedy. Today it receives an average 1.5 million visitors a year.

The popularity of Land Between the Lakes is easy to understand; there's something here for everyone who enjoys the great outdoors. Boating, fishing, hiking, horseback riding, swimming, bicycling, and wildlife viewing are a few of the outdoor activities available at LBL. Visitors can also see a working 1800s farm at the Homeplace Living History Farm, view the stars at the Golden Pond Planetarium, or learn more about the area at the Woodlands Nature Center. During the winter months, bald eagles can be spotted at LBL; some years as many as 150 eagles migrate here from northern areas. Elk and bison can be viewed year-round at the Elk and Bison Prairie.

Although there are camping opportunities at Land Between the Lakes in both Tennessee and Kentucky, this guide lists only the ones in Tennessee.

For more information:
Land Between the Lakes
Gold Pond Visitor Center
238 Visitor Center Dr.
Golden Pond, KY 42211-9001
(270) 924-2000
(800) 525-7077
landbetweenthelakes.us

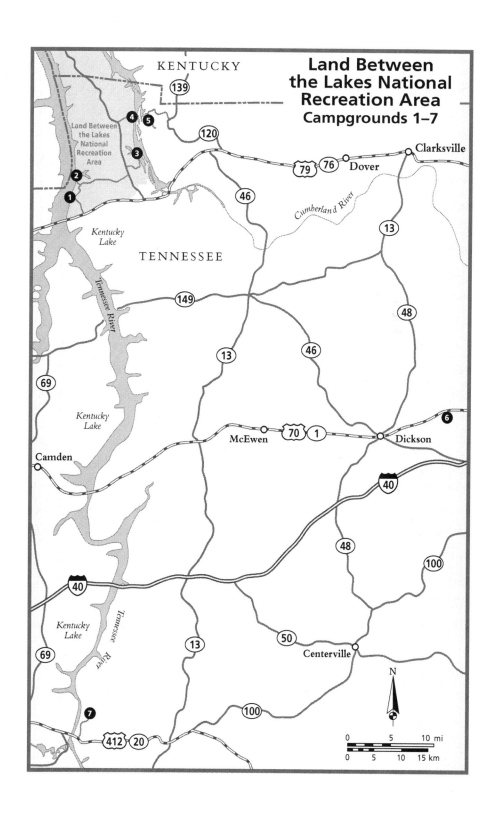

Land Between
the Lakes National
Recreation Area
Campgrounds 1–7

KENTUCKY

TENNESSEE

Land Between
the Lakes
National
Recreation
Area

Kentucky
Lake

Kentucky
Lake

Kentucky
Lake

Tennessee River

Cumberland River

Clarksville
Dover
Camden
McEwen
Dickson
Centerville

139
120
79 76
46
13
149
48
13 46
69
70 1
6
40
48
100
40
69 13
50
7
412 20
100

N

0   5   10 mi
0   5   10   15 km

Campground number	Campground	Group Sites	RV Sites	Total Sites	Max RV Length	Hookups	Toilets	Showers	Drinking water	Dump station	Pets	ADA Sites	Recreation	Fees ($)	Season	Can reserve	Stay limit (days)
1	Piney		328	384	60 ft	WES	F	•	•	•	•	•	FSHBLWP	$-$$$$	Mar–Nov	•	21
2	Boswell Landing			22	40 ft		V		•		•	•	FSBLWP	$-$$			14
3	Gatlin Point			19	25 ft		V		•		•	•	FBLW	$			14
4	Neville Bay	5		5			V				•		LBHWP	$			14
5	Bumpus Mills		15	15	64 ft	WE	F	•	•	•	•		BFSLP	$$$	May–Sept	•	14
6	Montgomery Bell State Park		72	94	60 ft	WES	F	•	•	•		•	BCLHFSP	$$$		•	14
7	Mousetail Landing State Park	2	25	48	52 ft	WE	F	•	•	•		•	SFBLHW	$-$$$		•	14

Hookups: W = Water   E = Electric   S = Sewer

Toilets: F = Flush   V = Vault   C = Chemical

Recreation: H = Hiking   S = Swimming   F = Fishing   B = Boating   L = Boat launch   R = Horseback riding   O = Off-road driving   W = Wildlife watching   M = Mountain biking   C = Rock climbing   G = Golf   P = Paddling

If no entry under Season, campground is open all year. If no entry under Fee, camping is free.

Campground Fee Ranges (per night): $ = $10 or less $$ = $11–$20 $$$ = $21–$30 $$$$ = $31 and above

1 Piney

Location: Land Between the Lakes, Kentucky Lake

GPS coordinates: 36.487 / -88.0345

Facilities and amenities: Tables, lantern poles, fire rings, grills; showers, flush toilets; laundry; dump station; electric, water, and sewer hookups; boat launch, beach

Elevation: 360 feet

Road conditions: Paved

Hookups: WES

Sites: 384

Maximum RV length: 60 feet

Season: Mar–Nov

Fee: $-$$$$

Maximum stay: 21 days

Management: USDA Forest Service; (931) 232-5331

Reservations: (800) 525-7077: usedirect.com/CampLBL

Pets: Yes

Quiet hours: 11 p.m.–6 a.m.

ADA compliant: Yes

Cell service: Good

Activities: Fishing, hunting, hiking, boating, paddling, water sports, swimming, bicycling, wildlife viewing

Finding the campground: From Dover take US 79 South approximately 12 miles and turn right onto Fort Henry Road. Go 2.5 miles; turn left at the campground sign and continue 0.2 mile to entrance.

About the campground: Piney is on the shores of Kentucky Lake (Tennessee River), and its location is very scenic. It offers 384 well-defined lakefront and wooded sites with 283 electric hookup sites; 44 sites with electric, water, and sewer; and 57 primitive sites. Most sites are capable of handling large motor homes and campers. Piney also has nineteen primitive cabins available for nightly rental. Campers have access to modern facilities, including a swimming beach, archery range, ball field, bike trails, a campfire theater, hiking trails, two boat ramps, and a fishing pier. In addition, the summer season offers weekend recreation programs for all ages.

2 Boswell Landing

Location: Land Between the Lakes, Kentucky Lake
GPS coordinates: 36.519 / -88.0245
Facilities and amenities: Tables, grills, fire rings; vault toilets; centrally located water; boat launch
Elevation: 406 feet
Road conditions: Paved and gravel
Hookups: None
Sites: 22
Maximum RV length: 40 feet
Season: Year-round
Fee: $-$$
Maximum stay: 14 days
Management: USDA Forest Service; (270) 924-2000
Reservations: No; first come, first served, self-service camping; walk up and pay on-site
Pets: Yes
Quiet hours: 11 p.m.–6 a.m.
ADA compliant: Yes
Cell service: Good
Activities: Fishing, hunting, hiking, boating, water sports, paddling, wildlife viewing
Finding the campground: From Dover, take US 79 South 10.7 miles to the Piney campground sign. Turn right at the sign onto FR 230 and go 4.5 miles to the Boswell Landing sign. Turn left at the sign onto FR 232 and continue 0.2 mile to a boat ramp sign. Turn right at the sign onto FR 233 (paved and gravel) and go 1 mile to the campground.
About the campground: Boswell Landing offers a primitive camping experience on Kentucky Lake. There are no hookups, and the sites do not have paved parking areas, but a small RV could park here. The sites are on a small rise overlooking Kentucky Lake. Boswell is not far from Piney on the same section of lake, but it gets fewer visitors because it's farther from the main road and has fewer amenities. This is a self-service camping area, with designated campsites that you pay for on-site.

3 Gatlin Point

Location: Land Between the Lakes, Lake Barkley
GPS coordinates: 36.5567 / -87.9035
Facilities and amenities: Tables, grills, fire rings; centrally located water; boat launch; vault toilets
Elevation: 453 feet
Road conditions: Gravel; some places narrow and rough
Hookups: None
Sites: 19
Maximum RV length: 25 feet
Season: Year-round
Fee: $
Maximum stay: 14 days
Management: USDA Forest Service; (270) 924-2000
Reservations: No; first come, first served, self-service camping; walk up and pay on-site
Pets: Yes
Quiet hours: 11 p.m.–6 a.m.
ADA compliant: Yes
Cell service: Spotty
Activities: Fishing, hunting, boating, water sports, wildlife viewing, hiking
Finding the campground: From Dover take US 79 South approximately 5 miles to the Land Between the Lakes sign. Turn right at the sign onto "The Trace" (TN 453) and go 4 miles to the Gatlin Point sign. Turn right after the sign onto FR 227 (gravel) and go 2.1 miles to T intersection. Turn left at the intersection onto FR 229 (gravel) and continue 1.6 miles to the campground, on the left.
About the campground: Gatlin Point is a lot like Boswell Campground—primitive and self-service camping. The parking sites are level and very shaded, and the section of Lake Barkley where it is located is peaceful. All the sites are primitive, with no hookups. About 0.25 mile from the campground is a bridge across the lake; this seems to be a good fishing spot, and we also spotted a bald eagle from here. For the person looking to get away from the crowds but still have a clean, organized campground, this is the place.

4 Neville Bay

Location: Land Between the Lakes, Lake Barkley
GPS coordinates: 36.614234 / -87.915847
Facilities and amenities: Tables; vault toilets
Elevation: 379 feet
Road conditions: Paved and gravel
Hookups: None
Sites: 5
Maximum RV length: N/A
Season: Year-round
Fee: $
Maximum stay: 14 days
Management: USDA Forest Service; (270) 924-2000
Reservations: No; dispersed camping; first come, first served. Anyone over the age of 18 needs a permit.
Pets: Yes
Quiet hours: 11 p.m.–6 a.m.
ADA compliant: Yes
Cell service: Spotty
Activities: Fishing, hunting, boating, hiking, water sports, wildlife viewing

Tent site at Land Between the Lakes

Finding the campground: From Dover take US 79 South approximately 5 miles. Watch for the sign and turn right onto "The Trace" (TN 453); continue 9.8 miles and turn right onto FR 214. Go 1.5 miles to Neville Bay. FR 214 is gravel but smooth and fairly wide.

About the campground: Neville is basically a lake-access area with dispersed camping allowed. There are no marked sites, just an open grassy area with a few picnic tables. You must obtain a permit for basic or dispersed camping for anyone over 18 years old. Permit options are $10 for a three-day permit or $50 for an annual permit.

5 Bumpus Mills

Location: Lake Barkley
GPS coordinates: 36.6185 / -87.8847
Facilities and amenities: Tables, grills; showers, flush toilets; dump station; electric and water hookups; playground, boat launch
Elevation: 466 feet
Road conditions: Paved
Hookups: WE
Sites: 15
Maximum RV length: 64 feet
Season: May–Sept
Fee: $$$
Maximum stay: 14 days
Management: US Army Corps of Engineers; (931) 232-8831
Reservations: (877) 444-6777; recreation.gov/camping/campgrounds/232537
Pets: Yes
Quiet hours: 10 p.m.–6 a.m.
ADA compliant: Yes
Cell service: Poor
Activities: Fishing, boating, water sports, swimming
Finding the campground: From Dover take US Highway 79 South approximately 3 miles; turn right at the campground sign onto TN 120 North. Go 10 miles; turn left onto Tobaccoport Road; continue 2.8 miles and turn left onto Oak Hill Road. Go 0.9 mile and turn left onto Forest Trail; continue 0.2 mile to the campground entrance.
About the campground: Bumpus Mills is a medium-size campground located in a beautiful setting of rolling hills next to Lake Barkley. The wooded sites are fairly good sized, accommodating most RVs. The campground has a nearby convenience store and public marina.

6 Montgomery Bell State Park

Location: West of Nashville

GPS coordinates: 36.0971 / -87.2861

Facilities and amenities: Tables, grills, fire rings; showers, flush toilets; centrally located drinking; water dump station; electric, water, and sewer hookups; playground

Elevation: 590 feet

Road conditions: Paved

Hookups: WES

Sites: 94

Maximum RV length: 60 feet

Season: Year-round

Fee: $$$

Maximum stay: 14 days

Management: Montgomery Bell State Park; (615) 797-9052

Reservations: reserve.tnstateparks.com/montgomery-bell/campsites

Pets: Yes

Quiet hours: 10 p.m.–6 a.m.

ADA compliant: Yes

Cell service: Good

Activities: Boating, fishing, canoeing, hiking, swimming, tennis, basketball, volleyball

Finding the campground: From the junction of US 70 and TN 96 in Dickson, take US 70 East for 3.7 miles. Watch for the sign; the park entrance is on the right. Follow the signs to the campground.

About the campground: Located only 40 minutes from downtown Nashville, Montgomery Bell State Park serves as a natural oasis for locals and travelers alike. The 3,850-acre park has three lakes that offer visitors the opportunity to soak up the sun on the swimming beach shores and paddle the calm waters. Open year-round, the campground provides 20/30/50-amp electric service and can accommodate 60-foot campers on most electrical sites. There are forty-seven sites equipped with water and electric; forty sites with on-site sewer and can accommodate pop-up campers to the largest RVs; and twenty-two tent-only campsites. There are two pull-through campsites accessible to persons with a disability. There are three bathhouses located in the campground. Picnic tables, trash cans, and grills are available at the campsites.

7 Mousetail Landing State Park

Location: Tennessee River/Kentucky Lake, east of Parsons
GPS coordinates: 35.6634 / -88.006
Facilities and amenities: Tables, grills, fire rings, lantern poles; showers, flush toilets; laundry; dump station; electric and water hookups; boat launch, archery range
Elevation: 590 feet
Road conditions: Paved
Hookups: WE
Sites: 48
Maximum RV length: 52 feet
Season: Year-round
Fee: $-$$$
Maximum stay: 14 days
Management: Mousetail Landing State Park; (901) 847-0841
Reservations: reserve.tnstateparks.com/mousetail-landing/campsites
Pets: Yes
Quiet hours: 10 p.m.–6 a.m.
ADA compliant: Yes
Cell service: Good
Activities: Boating, fishing, swimming, hiking, wildlife watching, volleyball, basketball, archery
Finding the campground: From the junction of US 412 and TN 69 in Parsons, take US 412 East approximately 6.5 miles. Turn left onto TN 438 East and go 2.5 miles; watch for the sign. The park entrance is on the left; follow signs to the campground.
About the campground: This 1,247-acre area is located on the banks of the Tennessee River. There are two different camping areas at the park. The main campground has twenty-five sites on a ridgetop above the river. These are more developed sites, with electric and water hookups. The sites in this section are good size with enough room for an RV and a second vehicle. The second camping area is known as the primitive area because the sites lack any sort of hookups. The sixteen primitive sites are next to the Tennessee River and have a boat launch. The primitive sites are as nice as the main campground, with large paved parking areas and plenty of room. The entrance to the primitive area is about 1.5 miles before you reach the main entrance. *Note:* The road drops off at this turn; caution is in order if you're pulling a low-clearance trailer.

Area 5: Shelbyville, Tim's Ford Lake, and Normandy Lake

The town of Shelbyville is famous for the Tennessee Walking Horse and is home to the Tennessee Walking Horse Celebration. This eleven-day event takes place annually in late August to early September. The celebration draws thousands of people each year, from Tennessee and abroad, who delight in the beauty of the Tennessee Walking Horse. Nearby Lynchburg is a small town well known as the home of the Jack Daniel's Distillery and Miss Mary Bobo's Southern-style restaurant.

Tim's Ford Lake, covering 11,950 acres, is one of the most picturesque lakes in Tennessee. It is a popular fishing destination for many anglers, with catches of smallmouth bass, walleye, crappie, and many other species. Tim's Ford is also a favorite spot in summer for people who enjoy water-related activities.

Normandy Dam, which creates Normandy Lake, is the largest non-power-generating TVA dam on any Tennessee River tributary. Normandy Dam was built in the mid-70s as a way of controlling floods, producing a water supply, and creating recreational opportunities. The dam also supplies water to the Normandy Fish Hatchery, one of the largest in the state. There are more than 500 species of fish in Normandy Lake.

For more information:
Shelbyville–Bedford County Chamber of Commerce
100 North Cannon Blvd.
Shelbyville 37160
(931) 684-3482
shelbyvilletn.com

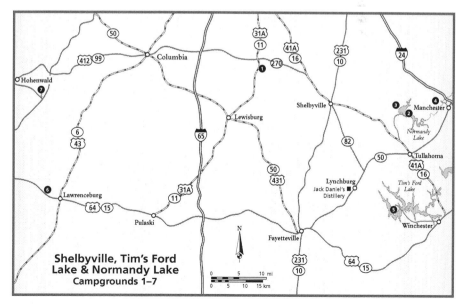

Shelbyville, Tim's Ford Lake & Normandy Lake
Campgrounds 1–7

Campground number	Campground	Group Sites	RV Sites	Total Sites	Max RV Length	Hookups	Toilets	Showers	Drinking water	Dump station	Pets	ADA Sites	Recreation	Fees ($)	Season	Can reserve	Stay limit (days)
1	Henry Horton State Park	3	54	84	65 ft	WE	F	•	•	•	•	•	HSGC	$-$$$$		•	14
2	Barton Springs		125	128	60 ft	WE	F	•	•	•	•	•	SBFLP	$$$$	Mar–Dec	•	Varies
3	Cedar Point		45	53	40 ft	WE	F	•	•	•	•	•	SBFLP	$$$-$$$$	Mar–Nov	•	Varies
4	Old Stone Fort State Park		50	50	50 ft	WE	F	•	•	•	•	•	HFWP	$$$-$$$$		•	14
5	Tim's Ford State Park	1	133	168	84 ft	WES	F	•	•	•	•	•	FHSGBLPW	$-$$$$		•	14-28
6	David Crockett State Park	1	97	107	55 ft	WE	F	•	•	•	•	•	HSFBLP	$$-$$$$		•	14
7	Meriwether Lewis Historic Site			32	36 ft		F		•			•	H				14

Hookups: W = Water   E = Electric   S = Sewer

Toilets: F = Flush   V = Vault   C = Chemical

Recreation: H = Hiking   S = Swimming   F = Fishing   B = Boating   L = Boat launch   R = Horseback riding   O = Off-road driving   W = Wildlife watching

M = Mountain biking   C = Rock climbing   G = Golf   P = Paddling

If no entry under Season, campground is open all year. If no entry under fee, camping is free.

Campground Fee Ranges (per night): $=$10 or less $$=$11-$20 $$$=$21-$30 $$$$=$31 and above

Tim's Ford Lake information:
(800) 238-2264

Normandy Lake information:
tva.com/energy/our-power-system/hydroelectric/normandy
tn.gov/twra/fishing/where-to-fish/middle-tennessee-r2/normandy-reservoir.
html

1 Henry Horton State Park

Location: Northwest of Shelbyville
GPS coordinates: 35.5916 / -86.702
Facilities and amenities: Tables, grills, fire rings; showers, flush toilets; dump station; electric and water hookups; playground
Elevation: 656 feet
Road conditions: Paved and smooth gravel
Hookups: WE
Sites: 84
Maximum RV length: 65 feet
Season: Year-round
Fee: $-$$$$
Maximum stay: 14 days
Management: Henry Horton State Park; (931) 364-2222
Reservations: reserve.tnstateparks.com/henry-horton/campsites
Pets: Yes
Quiet hours: 10 p.m.–6 a.m.
ADA compliant: Yes
Cell service: Good
Activities: Hiking, fishing, canoeing, swimming, paddling, golf, skeet shooting, volleyball
Finding the campground: From the junction of US 231 and US 41A in Shelbyville, take US 41A North 7.2 miles. Turn left onto TN 270 west and go 9.5 miles; turn left onto US 31A South and go 0.7 mile. The entrance to the campground is on the right.
About the campground: Henry Horton State Park was constructed in the 1960s on the estate of a former governor of Tennessee, Henry Horton. The park is located on the shores of the historic Duck River, one of the most diverse ecosystems in the world. Remnants of a mill and bridge operated and used by the family of Horton's spouse for more than a century may be seen today on the Wilhoite Mill Trail. The park offers several lodging options, including a lodge, eight cabins, fifty-four RV campsites, ten tent campsites, nine primitive campsites, six hammock campsites, three group campsites, and two backcountry campsites. The RV sites have water and electric hookups; all other sites do not. Hammock and backcountry sites are hike-in. Tent and primitive sites are drive-up and are well spaced out for privacy. The road into the primitive area is gravel. The sites in the modern RV area have paved pull-in sites; some are pull-through for RVs up to 65 feet. The park features the Restaurant and Lounge at Henry Horton, a destination for travelers as well as locals. A golf course, skeet-shooting range, swimming pool, and hiking trails are also contained on the park grounds.

2 Barton Springs

Location: Normandy Lake
GPS coordinates: 35.4544 / -86.2206
Facilities and amenities: Tables, grills; showers, flush toilets; dump station; electric and water hookups; boat launch
Elevation: 853 feet
Road conditions: Paved
Hookups: WE
Sites: 128
Maximum RV length: 60 feet
Season: Mar–Dec
Fee: $$$$
Maximum stay: Varies; 14 days to long-term
Management: Tennessee Valley Authority; (931) 857-9222
Reservations: reservations.camprrm.com/campground/13/pick_date
Pets: Yes
Quiet hours: 10 p.m.–6 a.m.
ADA compliant: Yes
Cell service: Good
Activities: Fishing, boating, paddling, water sports
Finding the campground: From the junction of US 41 and TN 269 in Tullahoma, take TN 269 North; this route is also known as Normandy Road West. Go 5.2 miles and turn right, crossing the

Old dam on Duck River, Old Stone Fort State Park

A picnic table near the lake at Barton Springs Campground

railroad tracks. After crossing the railroad tracks, bear left. There is no sign, but this is Frank Hiles Road; follow this 3 miles to the campground on the left.

About the campground: This is a great summertime spot for camping next to the water. Located on the shores of Normandy Lake, the campground has a total of 128 campsites. All sites have a lake view, and eleven sites are lakefront, offering the availability to fish from your campsite. There are forty-nine back-in sites, the remaining are gravel and pull-through; most sites are level. Each offers electric power of 50/30/20 amps and has a water faucet. A picnic table and fire pit/grill combo are at every site. The campground offers both short-term and long-term camping. There is good fishing here on the lake and good trout fishing at the base of Normandy Dam, where the waters are stocked.

3 Cedar Point

Location: Normandy Lake
GPS coordinates: 35.476 / -86.2277
Facilities and amenities: Tables, grills, fire ring; showers, flush toilets; dump station; electric and water hookups; general store, boat launch
Elevation: 885 feet
Road conditions: Paved
Hookups: WE
Sites: 53
Maximum RV length: 40 feet
Season: Mar–Nov
Fee: $$$–$$$$
Maximum stay: Varies; 14 days to long-term
Management: Tennessee Valley Authority; (931) 857-3705
Reservations: reservations.camprrm.com/campground/14/pick_date
Pets: Yes
Quiet hours: 10 p.m.–6 a.m.
ADA compliant: Yes
Cell service: Good
Activities: Fishing, boating, paddling, water sports
Finding the campground: From Manchester, follow US 41 North to Sixteenth Model Road and turn left. Go 4.3 miles and turn left on Roberts Ridge Road. Continue 3 miles and turn left onto Holland Hill Lane; after 0.2 mile turn right onto Cedar Point Road. The campground will be on the left after 1.6 miles.
About the campground: Cedar Point Campground lies on the Normandy TVA Reservoir and the upper Duck River. It is located in southern middle Tennessee between the towns of Normandy and Manchester. The nicely treed and grassy campground offers a secluded and quiet, family-oriented environment, and is surrounded by beautiful rolling hills and farmland. Cedar Point has a day-use area, a boat launch, and a small general store. A pavilion, which accommodates up to seventy-five people, may be reserved for a reasonable fee. The neighboring Barton Springs Campground, also managed by Recreation Resource Management, is located across the lake from Cedar Point.

4 Old Stone Fort State Park

Location: Manchester
GPS coordinates: 35.4922 / -86.1065
Facilities and amenities: Tables, grills, fire rings; showers, flush toilets; dump station; electric and water hookups
Elevation: 1,017 feet
Road conditions: Paved
Hookups: WE
Sites: 50
Maximum RV length: 50 feet
Season: Year-round
Fee: $$$–$$$$
Maximum stay: 14 days
Management: Old Stone Fort State Park; (615) 723-5073
Reservations: reserve.tnstateparks.com/old-stone-fort/campsites
Pets: Yes
Quiet hours: 10 p.m.–6 a.m.
ADA compliant: Yes
Cell service: Good
Activities: Hiking, fishing, paddling, wildlife viewing
Finding the campground: From I-24 in Manchester take exit 110 and go south on TN 53 for 0.9 mile. Turn right onto US 41N and go 0.7 mile. The park entrance is on the left; follow the signs to the campground.
About the campground: Old Stone Fort is a 2,000-year-old Native American ceremonial site that is fascinating to explore. The main hiking trail in the park follows the wall through dramatic scenery to the original entrance, which was designed to face the exact spot on the horizon where the sun rises during the summer solstice. A series of waterfalls on the Duck River draw both sightseers and photographers. Many of the campsites are located on the banks overlooking the river; all are spaced out with plenty of room and privacy.

5 Tim's Ford State Park

Location: Tim's Ford Lake
GPS coordinates: 35.2217 / -86.2513
Facilities and amenities: Tables, fire rings, grills; showers, flush toilets; laundry; dump station; electric, water, and sewer hookups; camp store, boat launch
Elevation: 951 feet
Road conditions: Paved
Hookups: WES
Sites: 168
Maximum RV length: 84 feet
Season: Year-round
Fee: $–$$$$
Maximum stay: 14 days, Mar–Nov; 28 days, Dec–Feb
Management: Tim's Ford State Park; (615) 967-4457
Reservations: reserve.tnstateparks.com/tims-ford/campsites
Pets: Yes
Quiet hours: 10 p.m.–6 a.m.
ADA compliant: Yes
Cell service: Spotty
Activities: Boating, paddling, swimming, water sports, fishing, hiking, bicycling, golf, hunting, wildlife viewing
Finding the campground: From Nashville, follow I-24 East to exit 111 at Manchester. Turn left onto TN 55 West into Tullahoma. Turn left onto TN 130 South. Follow TN 130 South to Awalt Road/TN 476 and turn right. Continue on Awalt Road/TN 476 until it dead-ends at Mansford Road/TN 476. Turn left onto Mansford Road/TN 476. The park entrance is 1.6 miles on the right.
About the campground: Located on the Tim's Ford Reservoir in south-central Tennessee, the 3,546-acre Tim's Ford State Park sits in the shadows of the Cumberland Plateau. Tim's Ford Lake is regarded as one of the top bass fishing and recreational lakes in the Southeast. Open year-round, the campground has 168 campsites across three areas (Main, Turkey Creek, and Fairview). There are fifty-two sites at the main campground with 30-amp electric service and water hookups. Four sites have sewer hookups. A dump station is located at the entrance to the campground for self-contained rigs. Two centrally located, heated bathhouses provide hot showers and bathrooms. Each site has a picnic table and a fire ring with a grill. A playground is located within the campground, and several other playgrounds are located throughout the park. The camp store is open year-round and Wi-Fi is available. There are eighty-two campsites at Fairview Campground; all have 20/30/50-amp electric and water hookups; sewer hookups are available at thirty-one sites. A dump station and bathhouse with hot showers are centrally located. Wi-Fi is available, and each site includes a table and fire ring with a grill. Turkey Creek is located 9 miles north of the main park. There are twenty primitive tent-only sites. Each site has a fire ring and picnic table, but there is no water or electricity. All offer a grassy surface. Showers and bathrooms are available at the campground. Additionally, for the adventurers, there are fourteen paddle- or hike-in backcountry campsites. These are primitive campsites with no amenities. Please practice Leave No Trace Principles and pack out what you pack in. This area is well known for the lake and fishing, but the park also offers 5 miles of paved trails for bicyclists and hikers, as well as a marina, bait shop, and rental boats.

6 David Crockett State Park

Location: Lawrenceburg
GPS coordinates: 35.2469 / -87.3508
Facilities and amenities: Tables, grills, fire rings; showers, flush toilets; dump station; recreation trail, boat launch
Elevation: 820 feet
Road conditions: Paved
Hookups: WE
Sites: 107
Maximum RV length: 55 feet
Season: Year-round
Fee: $$-$$$$
Maximum stay: 14 days
Management: David Crockett State Park; (615) 762-9408
Reservations: reserve.tnstateparks.com/david-crockett/campsites
Pets: Yes
Quiet hours: 10 p.m.-6 a.m.
ADA compliant: Yes
Cell service: Good
Activities: Hiking, fishing, swimming, boating, paddling; outdoor classroom
Finding the campground: From the junction of US 64 and US 43 in Lawrenceburg, take US 64 West 1.4 miles. The park entrance is on the right; follow the signs to the campground.
About the campground: Tennessee has two state parks named for David Crockett. The one mentioned earlier in this book is his birthplace; this is where he moved his family as an adult and set up his own business. At this location he established a powder mill, gristmill, and distillery on Shoal Creek—all of which were washed away by a flood in 1817. I enjoyed the campground here; its beautiful hilltop setting with plenty of shade is a great spot to camp in summer. The large sites are arranged in a way that makes it easy to park a large RV. Boats can be rented at 40-acre Lindsey Lake for fishing or just relaxing. The park also contains a restaurant and an outdoor classroom for learning more about the environment.

7 Meriwether Lewis Historic Site

Location: Natchez Trace Parkway near Hohenwald

GPS coordinates: 35.5225 / -87.456

Facilities and amenities: Tables, grills, fire rings; flush toilets; centrally located water

Elevation: 885 feet

Road conditions: Paved

Hookups: None

Sites: 32

Maximum RV length: 36 feet

Season: Year-round

Fee: None

Maximum stay: 14 days

Management: National Park Service; (800) 305-7417

Reservations: No; first come, first served

Pets: Yes

Quiet hours: 10 p.m.–6 a.m.

ADA compliant: Yes

Cell service: Poor

Activities: Hiking, cycling, historic learning

Finding the campground: The campground is located near mile marker 386 on the Natchez Trace Parkway, at the Meriwether Lewis Historic Site. If you're coming from Hohenwald, take TN 20 East for 7 miles to the parkway; the campground is at the junction of TN 20 and the parkway.

About the campground: The National Park Service manages three campgrounds along the 444-mile Natchez Trace Parkway. This is a simple, primitive camping area with no hookups. However, it is a good place to spend the night if you're traveling the Natchez Trace Parkway and do not wish to wander far off the road. Don't be fooled by this being a primitive campground, though; it's very orderly and well kept—located atop beautiful rolling ridges beneath a canopy of hardwood trees. There are a few pull-through sites, and most will accommodate a 36-foot RV. Its location next to the site of Meriwether Lewis's grave and the place where he met his untimely death make this a fascinating area for exploring a piece of American history. Cycling is a popular activity along the Natchez Trace.

West Tennessee

Area 1: Reelfoot Lake and Kentucky Lake

Reelfoot Lake is a truly amazing place, and the way it was created is equally impressive. An earthquake that shook the Mississippi River Valley in 1811 created a depression that soon filled with water, forming the lake we now know as Reelfoot. Today the lake is both an important wetland area for waterfowl and wildlife and a recreation area for visitors. Thousands of ducks and geese winter here each year, but Reelfoot is best known for its winter bald eagle population. Each year 100 to 200 bald eagles migrate from northern states to Reelfoot to spend the winter. Eagle tours are conducted at several locations during the winter months. Reelfoot is also a popular hunting and fishing area that first drew such hunters as Jim Bowie and Davy Crockett.

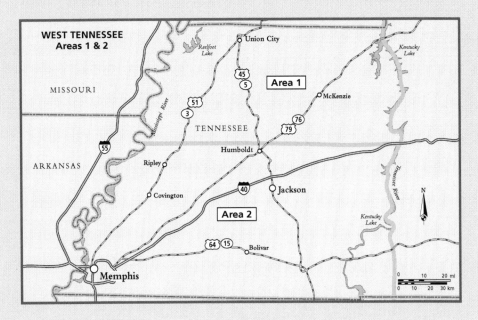

Kentucky Lake is the largest man-made lake in the eastern United States and one of the largest in the entire country. Its 160,000 acres of water and more than 2,000 miles of shoreline make it a premier outdoor playground and recreational area. The lake was created when the Tennessee Valley Authority (TVA) built a dam on the Tennessee River in Kentucky to control flooding on the lower Ohio and Mississippi Rivers; the resulting lake is a mecca for fishing and other water recreation. Although the dam is located in Kentucky, the lake itself stretches from Kentucky south halfway across Tennessee.

For more information:
Northwest Tennessee Tourism
PO Box 807
Paris 38242
(866) 698-6386
northwesttennesseetourism.com

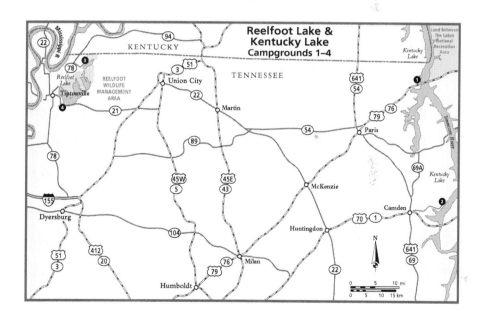

Campground number	Campground	Group Sites	RV Sites	Total Sites	Max RV Length	Hookups	Toilets	Showers	Drinking water	Dump station	Pets	ADA Sites	Recreation	Fees ($)	Season	Can reserve	Stay limit (days)
1	Paris Landing State Park		45	57	95 ft	WE	F	•	•	•	•	•	HFSBP	$$-$$$		•	14
2	Nathan Bedford Forrest State Park	1	37	61	68 ft	WE	F	•	•	•	•	•	HFSBP			•	14
3	Reelfoot Lake State Park—Airpark North		14	14	66 ft	WE	F	•	•	•	•	•	HFBWP	$$$		•	14
4	Reelfoot Lake State Park—South		88	88	70 ft	WE	F	•	•	•	•	•	HFBWP	$$$-$$$$		•	14

Hookups: W = Water   E = Electric   S = Sewer

Toilets: F = Flush   V = Vault   C = Chemical

Recreation: H = Hiking   S = Swimming   F = Fishing   B = Boating   L = Boat launch   R = Horseback riding   O = Off-road driving   W = Wildlife watching   M = Mountain biking   C = Rock climbing   G = Golf   P = Paddling

If no entry under Season, campground is open all year. If no entry under Fee, camping is free

Campground Fee Ranges (per night): $=$10 or less $$=$11-$20 $$$=$21-$30 $$$$=$31 and above

1 Paris Landing State Park

Location: Kentucky Lake
GPS coordinates: 36.4401 / -88.0845
Facilities and amenities: Tables, grills, fire rings, lantern poles; showers, flush toilets; laundry; dump station; water and electric hookups; boat launch, restaurant
Elevation: 360 feet
Road conditions: Paved
Hookups: WE
Sites: 57
Maximum RV length: 95 feet
Season: Year-round
Fee: $$–$$$
Maximum stay: 14 days
Management: Paris Landing State Park; (731) 641-4465
Reservations: reserve.tnstateparks.com/paris-landing
Pets: Yes
Quiet hours: 10 p.m.–6 a.m.
ADA compliant: Yes
Cell service: Good
Activities: Fishing, swimming, boating, water sports, paddling, hiking, golf
Finding the campground: From Paris, take US 79 North for approximately 16 miles. Just before you cross Kentucky Lake, the entrance to the campground is on the left.

Angler leaving the dock, Paris Landing State Park

About the campground: Paris Landing State Park is an 841-acre park located on the western shore of the Tennessee River, which is dammed to form Kentucky Lake (160,000 acres). The park sits on the widest part of the lake, making it the perfect location for water sports such as fishing, boating, and water-skiing. The park also offers a beautiful and challenging par 72, eighteen-hole golf course. The park pro shop provides golfing supplies, lessons, rental clubs, and carts. Paris Landing got its name from its location on the Tennessee River. Where the park is now located was a major steamboat port during the 1800s, bringing supplies to the town of Paris. The landing is now a wonderful recreational area. The beautifully landscaped campground, adjacent to the marina and boat launch area, is divided into two sections: an eighteen-site primitive area that offers basic camping and a forty-five-site area with paved sites and hookups. A short distance on the other side of TN 79 is the rest of the park, with a swimming pool, golf course, and restaurant.

2 Nathan Bedford Forrest State Park

Location: Kentucky Lake
GPS coordinates: 36.0921 / -87.9864
Facilities and amenities: Tables, grills; showers, flush toilets; dump station; water and electric hookups; boat launch
Elevation: 393 feet
Road conditions: Paved
Hookups: WE
Sites: 61
Maximum RV length: 68 feet
Season: Year-round
Fee: $–$$$$
Maximum stay: 14 days
Management: Nathan Bedford Forrest State Park; (731) 584-6356
Reservations: reserve.tnstateparks.com/nathan-bedford-forrest/campsites
Pets: Yes
Quiet hours: 10 p.m.–6 a.m.
ADA compliant: Yes
Cell service: Spotty
Activities: Swimming, fishing, boating, paddling, water sports, hiking
Finding the campground: From the junction of US 70 and US 641 in Camden, take US 70 East 1 mile to TN 191. Take TN 191 North through downtown, following the signs 7.9 miles to the park entrance.
About the campground: Nathan Bedford Forrest State Park began as a local park constructed by the Works Progress Administration (WPA), a Depression-era work recovery program. Now, as a Tennessee State Park, it is home to the Tennessee River Folklife Interpretive Center and Museum, situated on one of the highest points in West Tennessee, Pilot Knob. The park contains more than 20 miles of hiking trails. The main campground at Nathan Bedford is situated between two hills in a quiet hollow known as Happy Hollow. A small stream flows through the campground. There are thirty-seven sites, each equipped with tables, grills, and water and electric hookups. A central bathhouse with hot showers and a dump station are available. The Lakefront campground is primitive camping with thirteen sites that has centrally located water and restroom. Backcountry and group camping are also available.

3 Reelfoot Lake State Park–Airpark North

Location: Reelfoot Lake
GPS coordinates: 36.4737 / -89.3435
Facilities and amenities: Tables, grills; showers, flush toilets; dump station; water and electric hookups
Elevation: 262
Road conditions: Paved
Hookups: WE
Sites: 14
Maximum RV length: 66 feet
Season: Year-round
Fee: $$$
Maximum stay: 14 days
Management: Reelfoot Lake State Park; (731) 253-7756
Reservations: reserve.tnstateparks.com/reelfoot-lake/campsites
Pets: Yes
Quiet hours: 10 p.m.–6 a.m.
ADA compliant: Yes
Cell service: Spotty
Activities: Boating, fishing, hiking, hunting, wildlife watching
Finding the campground: From the junction of TN 78 and TN 21 in Tiptonville, take TN 78 North 7.7 miles and turn right onto TN 213 East. Go 3.2 miles; the road ends at the campground.
The campground: The Airpark North Campground at Reelfoot Lake State Park gets its name from the fact that it is located next to a small landing strip. The landing strip is not that busy and doesn't really disturb the campground. The campground is also next to the Airpark Inn and Restaurant at Reelfoot Lake. The campground is very open, with mostly small trees for shade and lots of grassy areas for kids to play. This is not a wilderness experience, but it's a good location for accessing the lake and watching the eagles. There is a boat launch just off TN 213, about 2 miles from the campground.

4 Reelfoot Lake State Park–South

Location: Reelfoot Lake
GPS coordinates: 36.3543 / -89.3962
Facilities and amenities: Tables, grills; showers, flush toilets; laundry; dump station; water and electric hookups; boat launch
Elevation: 262 feet
Road conditions: Paved
Hookups: WE
Sites: 88
Maximum RV length: 70 feet
Season: Year-round
Fee: $$$–$$$$
Maximum stay: 14 days
Management: Reelfoot Lake State Park; (731) 253-9652
Reservations: reserve.tnstateparks.com/reelfoot-lake/campsites
Pets: Yes
Quiet hours: 10 p.m.–6 a.m.
ADA compliant: Yes
Cell service: Spotty
Activities: Boating, fishing, hiking, hunting, wildlife watching
Finding the campground: From the junction of TN 78 and TN 21 in Tiptonville, take TN 21 East 5.4 miles; the campground entrance is on the left.
About the campground: This campground is located next to the visitor center for Reelfoot Lake State Park. It, too, is not in a wilderness setting but is located near stores and other facilities. It is, however, on the shores of Reelfoot Lake, and despite its location near commercialization, it's a very peaceful place to camp and to base a fishing trip. The sites are level with lots of room and shade from large hardwood trees. Fish-cleaning stations are provided throughout the campground, and local guide services are available nearby.

Area 2: Memphis and Jackson

There are two sizable towns in the southwest corner of Tennessee—Memphis and Jackson, both full of art, culture, and history. Memphis is located in the southwest tip of the state, perched on the Chickasaw Bluffs overlooking the mighty Mississippi River. It is bordered on the west by Arkansas and by Mississippi to the south. Memphis is the second-largest city in Tennessee behind Nashville and is well known as the birthplace of blues, soul, and rock and roll—home to the "King of Rock and Roll," Elvis Presley, Graceland, barbecue, Beale Street, and the Blues Hall of Fame. Memphis is also home to Tennessee's largest African American population and was the site of Martin Luther King Jr.'s 1968 assassination. The city now hosts the National Civil Rights Museum. Memphis is a city with many influences and styles; there is something here for every taste and interest.

Jackson, located 70 miles east of Memphis, was occupied by the Chickasaw people at the time of European encounter. They were pushed out by European-American settlers under the Indian Removal Act of 1830. The European-American settlement of Jackson began along the Forked Deer River in 1821 and was first named Alexandria. The name was changed in 1822 to honor Andrew Jackson, who later became our nation's seventh president. Davy Crockett, who traveled extensively around Tennessee, at one time made Jackson his home. It was here in Jackson, after losing his bid for reelection to Congress, that he gave a speech that produced one of his most famous quotes: "You can go to hell, I'm going to Texas." As of 2020, Jackson had a population of 68,205.

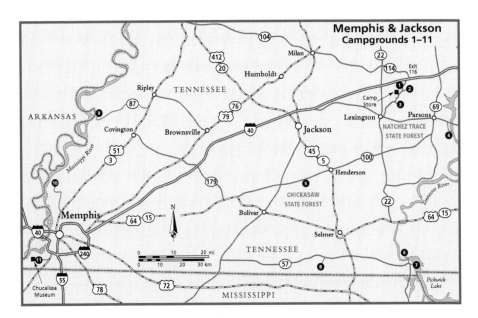

Campground number	Campground	Group Sites	RV Sites	Total Sites	Max RV Length	Hookups	Toilets	Showers	Drinking water	Dump station	Pets	ADA Sites	Recreation	Fees ($)	Season	Can reserve	Stay limit (days)
1	Natchez Trace State Park—Wrangler Campground		62	62	90 ft	WE	F	•	•	•	•	•	HR	$$$		•	14
2	Natchez Trace State Park—Cub Lake Campgrounds One and Two	3	40	43	25 ft	WE	F	•	•	•	•	•	FHP	$$$		•	14
3	Natchez Trace—Pin Oak Campground		77	77	80 ft	WES	F	•	•	•	•	•	FSHP	$$$$		•	14
4	Decatur County Beech Bend Park	4	63	74	None	WE	F	•	•	•	•	•	FSP	$$$		•	None
5	Chickasaw State Park		52	115	115 ft	WE	F	•	•	•	•	•	HFBPR	$$-$$$$		•	14
6	Pickwick Dam		85	93	78 ft	WE	F	•	•	•	•	•	HFBP	$$-$$$	Mar-Nov	•	21
7	Pickwick Landing State Park		48	86	72 ft	WES	F	•	•	•	•	•	HFBPSG	$-$$$		•	14
8	Big Hill Pond State Park		28	28	70 ft	WE	F	•	•	•	•	•	HFBPROM	$$		•	14
9	Fort Pillow State Park		32	33	60 ft	WE	F	•	•	•	•	•	HFWBP	$-$$$		•	14
10	Meeman-Shelby Forest State Park	1	48	49	48 ft	WE	F	•	•	•	•	•	HFSMP	$$$		•	14
11	T. O. Fuller State Park		45	45	85 ft	WE	F	•	•	•	•	•	HSG	$$$		•	14

Hookups: W = Water   E = Electric   S = Sewer

Toilets: F = Flush   V = Vault   C = Chemical

Recreation: H = Hiking   S = Swimming   F = Fishing   B = Boating   L = Boat launch   R = Horseback riding   O = Off-road driving   W = Wildlife watching   M = Mountain biking   C = Rock climbing
G = Golf   P = Paddling

If no entry under Season, campground is open all year. If no entry under Fee, camping is free.

Campground Fee Ranges (per night): $=$10 or less $$=$11–$20 $$$=$21–$30 $$$$=$31 and above

For more information:
Memphis Area
Chamber of Commerce
22 North Front St. #200
Memphis 38101
(901) 543-3500
memphischamber.com

Memphis Tourism
46 Union Ave.
Memphis 38103
(901) 543-5300
memphistravel.com/camping

Tennessee State Welcome Center
119 North Riverside Dr.
Memphis 38101
(901) 543-5333

Jackson Chamber of Commerce
197 Auditorium St.
PO Box 1904
Jackson 38302-1904
(731) 423-2200
jacksontn.com

Note: There are four campgrounds at Natchez Trace State Park. Campgrounds One and Two are next to each other; the Wrangler and Pin Oak Campgrounds are several miles apart.

1 Wrangler Campground, Natchez Trace State Park

Location: East of Jackson
GPS coordinates: 35.7923 / -88.2711
Facilities and amenities: Tables, grills, fire rings, lantern poles; showers, flush toilets; dump station; water and electric hookups
Elevation: 656 feet
Road conditions: Paved
Hookups: WE
Sites: 62
Maximum RV length: 90 feet
Season: Year-round
Fee: $$$
Maximum stay: 14 days
Management: Natchez Trace State Park; (731) 968-3742
Reservations: reserve.tnstateparks.com/natchez-trace/campsites
Pets: Yes
Quiet hours: 10 p.m.–6 a.m.
ADA compliant: Yes
Cell service: Spotty
Activities: Hiking, horseback riding
Finding the campground: From I-40, take exit 116 and go south on TN 114, also known as Natchez Trace Road, for 2.3 miles. The campground entrance is on the right.
About the campground: The name of this campground comes from the fact that it is next to the riding stables, and some of the sites have tie-outs for horses. The campground is well spaced into three separate areas. Campers must clean up after their own horses, which helps maintain a clean camping area. Sites 35 to 62 have more room for a larger RV or trailer. There are nearby lakes for fishing and trails for hiking.

2 Cub Lake Campgrounds One and Two, Natchez Trace State Park

Location: East of Jackson
GPS coordinates: 35.7761 / -88.2552
Facilities and amenities: Tables, grills, lantern poles; showers, flush toilets; dump station; water and electric hookups
Elevation: 524 feet
Road conditions: Paved
Hookups: WE
Sites: 43
Maximum RV length: Campground One, 25 feet; Campground Two, 20 feet
Season: Year-round
Fee: $$$
Maximum stay: 14 days
Management: Natchez Trace State Park; (731) 968-3742
Reservations: reserve.tnstateparks.com/natchez-trace/campsites
Pets: Yes
Quiet hours: 10 p.m.–6 a.m.
ADA compliant: Yes
Cell service: Good
Activities: Fishing, hiking, paddling
Finding the campground: From I-40, take exit 116 and go south on TN 114, also known as Natchez Trace Road. The road forks at the park store; stay to the left on Parson's Road for a total of 5.5 miles to the entrance to Campgrounds One and Two.
About the campground: Cub Lake Campground One has twenty-three sites and one bathhouse. The sites feature 20-, 30-amp electric; sites 8, 9, 11, and 12 have 50-amp electric. All sites have water hookups, and there is a dump station. There is a strict RV size restriction of 25 feet and under. This campground is open seasonally. Cub Lake Campground Two has twenty individual sites, three group sites, a bathhouse, and a dump station. The sites are primarily primitive. Water is available at the bathhouse but not at all campsites. There is a strict RV size restriction of under 20 feet. The campground is open seasonally.

3 Pin Oak Campground, Natchez Trace State Park

Location: East of Jackson
GPS coordinates: 35.6935 / -88.2911
Facilities and amenities: Tables, grills, fire rings; showers, flush toilets; laundry; water, electric, and sewer hookups at all sites; boat launch
Elevation: 459 feet
Road conditions: Paved
Hookups: WES
Sites: 77
Maximum RV length: 80 feet
Season: Year-round
Fee: $$$$
Maximum stay: 14 days
Management: Natchez Trace State Park; (731) 968-3742
Reservations: reserve.tnstateparks.com/natchez-trace/campsites
Pets: Yes
Quiet hours: 10 p.m.–6 a.m.
ADA compliant: Yes
Cell service: Poor
Activities: Hiking, fishing
Finding the campground: From I-40, take exit 116 and go south on TN 114, also known as Natchez Trace Road. The road forks at the park store; stay to the right on TN 114 for approximately 7.5 miles. Turn left at the sign for the campground onto an unsigned road and continue 2.7 miles to the campground entrance.
About the campground: Pin Oak is situated on a small hill overlooking Pin Oak Lake and is best for large RVs up to 80 feet. The campground has seventy-seven sites, two bathhouses, and 50-amp electric, sewer, and water hookups. The RV camp also offers a swimming beach, playground, picnic shelter, camping cabins, and a boat dock. While this campground is open year-round, some campsites close after December 1. Campers should be aware that there is very limited, if any, cell service available in the Pin Oak campground area.

4 Decatur County Beech Bend Park

Location: Tennessee River/Kentucky Lake, east of Parsons
GPS coordinates: 35.6122 / -88.0402
Facilities and amenities: Tables, grills, fire rings, lantern poles; showers, flush toilets; dump station; water and electric hookups; boat launch
Elevation: 360 feet
Road conditions: Paved
Hookups: WE
Sites: 74
Maximum RV length: No limit
Season: Year-round
Fee: $$$
Maximum stay: No limit
Management: Decatur County Parks & Recreation; (731) 733-3305
Reservations: No; first come, first served
Pets: Yes
Quiet hours: 10 p.m.–6 a.m.
ADA compliant: Yes
Cell service: Good
Activities: Fishing, boating, swimming, paddling, water sports
Finding the campground: From the junction of TN 69 and US 412 in Parsons, take US 412 East 4.6 miles and turn right onto TN 100W. Go 1.6 miles; the campground entrance is on the left.
About the campground: Beech Bend Park is a well-kept county campground. This level camping area sits back on a slough just off the main channel of the Tennessee River. A boat launch ramp allows campers to take advantage of the good fishing. Reservations are not accepted, and there is no limit on the number of days you can camp.

5 Chickasaw State Park

Location: West of Henderson
GPS coordinates: 35.3943 / -88.7716
Facilities and amenities: Tables, grills, fire rings; showers, flush toilets; dump station; water and electric hookups; beach
Elevation: 590 feet
Road conditions: Paved
Hookups: WE
Sites: 115
Maximum RV length: 115 feet
Season: Year-round; tent camping area closed in winter
Fee: $$-$$$$
Maximum stay: 14 days
Management: Chickasaw State Park; (731) 989-5141
Reservations: reserve.tnstateparks.com/chickasaw/campsites
Pets: Yes
Quiet hours: 10 p.m.–6 a.m.
ADA compliant: Yes
Cell service: Good
Activities: Fishing, swimming, paddleboats, golf, hiking, horseback riding, tennis, basketball
Finding the campground: From the junction of TN 365 and TN 100 in Henderson, take TN 100 West 8.3 miles. Turn left at the sign for the park entrance and follow the signs to the campground.
About the campground: Chickasaw State Park was named for the Chickasaw Tribe who once inhabited West Tennessee and North Mississippi. There are three camping areas at Chickasaw State Park, and all three are very close to one another. A twenty-nine-site tent area at the lakeside is closed in winter. These have water but no electric hookups. The sites here are rather secluded, set within the forest and providing a good feeling of privacy. The riding stables and wranglers camping area are a short distance away. Thirty-one sites here offer water and electric hookups for RVs. These sites are for those folks who want to be near their horses. There are more than 100 miles of horseback trails in the Chickasaw State Forest, and you can bring your own horse or hire one from the stables. It's a nice, level area—very open with lots of grass and shaded by tall, majestic pine trees. The RV section is only a few hundred yards away and has fifty-two sites spaced out around a slight hillside. The RV sites have water and electric hookups, and even though they are called RV sites, tents are welcome. All three areas are within walking distance of one another and the activities in the park.

6 Pickwick Dam

Location: Tennessee River/Pickwick Lake
GPS coordinates: 35.0669 / -88.2603
Facilities and amenities: Tables, grills, fire rings, lantern poles; showers, flush toilets; dump station; water and electric hookups; boat launch
Elevation: 360 feet
Road conditions: Paved
Hookups: WE
Sites: 93
Maximum RV length: 78 feet
Season: Mar–Nov
Fee: $$–$$$
Maximum stay: 21 days
Management: Tennessee Valley Authority; (256) 386-2006
Reservations: (865) 361-9492; reservations.camprrm.com/campground/6/pick_date
Pets: Yes
Quiet hours: 10 p.m.–6 a.m.
ADA compliant: Yes
Cell service: Good
Activities: Fishing, boating, paddling, hiking
Finding the campground: From the junction of TN 45 and TN 57 in Eastview, take TN 57 East 19 miles. Just after crossing Pickwick Dam, turn left onto Sportsman Road; follow the signs to the campground.
About the campground: The campground here is just a few hundred yards downstream from the dam. The sites are not on the banks of the river but just across the road. A boat launch and river access are at the entrance to the campground. The campground is shaded by tall, mature pine trees that litter the ground with pine needles and give this area a wonderful feel and smell. All the sites are level and will accommodate large RVs or tents; eight sites are primitive and have no hookups. There are more recreational opportunities a short distance away at Pickwick Landing State Park.

7 Pickwick Landing State Park

Location: Pickwick Lake/Tennessee River
GPS coordinates: 35.0521 / -88.2425
Facilities and amenities: Tables, grills, fire rings; showers, flush toilets; dump station; water, electric, and some sewer hookups; marina and boat launch
Elevation: 426 feet
Road conditions: Paved
Hookups: WES
Sites: 86
Maximum RV length: 72 feet
Season: Year-round
Fee: $–$$$
Maximum stay: 14 days
Management: Pickwick Landing State Park; (800) 250-8615
Reservations: reserve.tnstateparks.com/pickwick-landing/campsites
Pets: Yes
Quiet hours: 10 p.m.–6 a.m.
ADA compliant: Yes
Cell service: Good
Activities: Fishing, boating, paddling, water sports, swimming, hiking, golf, tennis
Finding the campground: From the junction of TN 45 and TN 57 in Eastview, take TN 57 East 18.2 miles. At the intersection, TN 57 turns right; the park entrance is on the left just after this turn.
About the campground: Pickwick Landing State Park is one of Tennessee's resort parks, with luxury-style accommodations and a multitude of recreational opportunities for families and individuals. Accommodations in the park include a large marina, a lodge, nice restaurant, cabins, and camping. In addition to water sports, guests enjoy golfing, birding, picnicking, disc golf, nature walks, and tennis. The main campground is located within walking distance of the marina, and there are slips available for private boats. This is a great family campground. Sites are varied in size for both tents and RVs, and some have full hookups. The main campground has forty-eight sites, each equipped with a table, a grill, and electrical and water hookups. Bathhouse and dump station are centrally located. Open year-round. Fourteen sites have 20/30/50-amp electric, and the two ADA-compliant sites have 20/30-amp electric. Bruton Branch Recreation Area is a primitive campground and picnic area located on the north side of Pickwick Lake. The campground has thirty-three sites, most of which are located on the lake. There are no electric or water hookups at these campsites, but there is a bathhouse with showers and potable water. The park has a large marina, a nice restaurant, and a challenging golf course.

8 Big Hill Pond State Park

Location: Pocahontas
GPS coordinates: 35.0656 / -88.7224
Facilities and amenities: Tables, grills, fire rings; showers, flush toilets; centrally located water; boat launch
Elevation: 524 feet
Road conditions: Paved
Hookups: None
Sites: 28
Maximum RV length: 70 feet
Season: Year-round
Fee: $$
Maximum stay: 14 days
Management: Big Hill Pond State Park; (731) 645-7967
Reservations: reserve.tnstateparks.com/big-hill-pond/campsites
Pets: Yes
Quiet hours: 10 p.m.–6 a.m.
ADA compliant: Yes
Cell service: Good
Activities: Fishing, boating, hiking, horseback riding; off-roading and mountain biking on the back roads
Finding the campground: From the junction of TN 45 and TN 57 in Eastview, take TN 57 West 10.7 miles. The park entrance is on the left; follow the signs to the campground.
About the campground: Big Hill Pond State Park is named for the 35-acre pond that is accessed by a four-wheel-drive road, but Travis McNatt Lake is not far from the campground. This lake is accessed by paved road; there is a boat launch available for small motorboats. Visitors can enjoy camping, hiking, birding, off-roading, mountain biking, fishing, and paddling. The park is home to 30 miles of overnight and day-use trails, with four backpack trail shelters. Big Hill Pond has twenty-eight tent and small RV campsites. Most sites will accommodate a trailer up to 20 feet. Each site has a table and a grill. The campground has a modern bathhouse with hot showers but no hookups, and there is no dump station. Because the campground is small, generators are not allowed after 10 p.m.

9 Fort Pillow State Park

Location: Mississippi River
GPS coordinates: 35.6282 / -89.8551
Facilities and amenities: Tables, grills, fire rings; showers, flush toilets, centrally located water; laundry
Elevation: 393 feet
Road conditions: Paved to gravel
Hookups: WE
Sites: 33
Maximum RV length: 60 feet
Season: Year-round
Fee: $-$$$
Maximum stay: 14 days
Management: Fort Pillow State Park; (731) 738-5581
Reservations: reserve.tnstateparks.com/fort-pillow/campsites
Pets: Yes
Quiet hours: 10 p.m.–6 a.m.
ADA compliant: Yes
Cell service: Good
Activities: Fishing, boating, hiking, wildlife watching
Finding the campground: From the junction of TN 87 and US 51, take TN 87 West 17.5 miles. Turn right onto TN 207 North and go 1 mile to the park entrance; follow the signs to the campground.
About the campground: Located approximately 40 miles north of Memphis, Fort Pillow State Historic Park is rich in historic and archaeological significance. Steep bluffs overlooking the Mississippi River made this area a strategic location during the Civil War. The fort was originally built by Confederate troops in 1861 and named for General Gideon J. Pillow of Maury County. It was abandoned in 1862 due to the Union Navy's advancement along the Mississippi River. The area became a state park in 1971. The Family Campground has six campsites that accommodate RVs and campers with 20/30/50-amp electrical and water hookups. The six sites accommodate rigs up to 60 feet. There are fifteen sites with 20-amp electric hookups and water stations in close proximity to each site. The 15-acre Fort Pillow Lake is stocked with bass, bream, crappie, and catfish. A boat launch is provided, but only electric motors are allowed.

10 Meeman-Shelby Forest State Park

Location: Mississippi River
GPS coordinates: 35.3461 / -90.0448
Facilities and amenities: Tables, grills, fire rings; showers, flush toilets; dump station; water and electric hookups; boat launch
Elevation: 360 feet
Road conditions: Paved
Hookups: WE
Sites: 49
Maximum RV length: 48 feet
Season: Year-round
Fee: $$$
Maximum stay: 14 days
Management: Meeman-Shelby State Park; (901) 876-5215
Reservations: reserve.tnstateparks.com/meeman-shelby-forest/campsites
Pets: Yes
Quiet hours: 10 p.m.–6 a.m.
ADA compliant: Yes
Cell service: Good
Activities: Fishing, swimming, paddling, hiking, bicycling, disc golf course
Finding the campground: From I-40 in Memphis, take exit 2A and go north on US Highway 51 for 2.7 miles. Turn left onto TN 388N and go 8 miles; turn left onto Locke-Cuba Road and go 0.7 mile. Turn right on Bluff Road; continue 0.8 mile and turn left into the park entrance. Follow the signs to the campground.
About the campground: The 12,539-acre Meeman-Shelby Forest State Park borders the mighty Mississippi River 13 miles north of Memphis and features a mature bald cypress and tupelo swamp. The park campground provides forty-nine campsites equipped with table, grill, and electrical and water hookups and one group camp available to youth groups that can accommodate up to 140 persons. This campground provides a great rural escape from the city of Memphis. The road through the campground has been newly repaved and is very wide, making it perfect for RVs. The campground is located on the Chickasaw Bluffs overlooking the Mississippi River, and a scenic road winds its way down from the campground to the river. Boats can be launched onto the Mississippi here. The park also has two small lakes, Poplar Tree and Piersol. Poplar Tree Lake is 125 acres and is good for fishing. Johnboats can be rented, or personal boats can be used on Poplar Tree Lake for a small fee (electric motors only).

11 T. O. Fuller State Park

Location: Memphis city limits
GPS coordinates: 35.0605 / -90.1258
Facilities and amenities: Tables, grills, fire rings, lantern poles; showers, flush toilets; dump station; water and electric hookups; swimming pool, ball fields, basketball and tennis courts, archery range
Elevation: 295 feet
Road conditions: Paved
Hookups: WE
Sites: 45
Maximum RV length: 85 feet
Season: Year-round
Fee: $$$
Maximum stay: 14 days
Management: T. O. Fuller State Park; (901) 543-7581
Reservations: https://reserve.tnstateparks.com/t-o-fuller/campsites
Pets: Yes
Quiet hours: 10 p.m.–6 a.m.
ADA compliant: Yes
Cell service: Good
Activities: Hiking, swimming, tennis, basketball, archery
Finding the campground: From I-55/240 in Memphis, take exit 7 and go south on US 61 for 1.6 miles. Turn right onto Mitchell Road and continue 3.2 miles to the park entrance. Follow the signs to the campground.
About the campground: T. O. Fuller State Park was the first state park open for African Americans east of the Mississippi River. It was designated Shelby County Negro State Park in 1938 and changed to T. O. Fuller State Park in 1942 in honor of Dr. Thomas O. Fuller, a prominent African American educator, pastor, politician, civic leader, and author who spent his life empowering and educating African Americans. This is the only state park within the city limits of Memphis, making it a great spot for campers who want to be close to downtown Memphis and its many tourist sites. The campground has many hardwood trees that provide plenty of shade. Forty-five campsites are RV accessible, with some sites accommodating rigs up to 85 feet. Tent campers are also welcome. The campground has a picnic shelter, playground, bathhouse, and laundry. Each campsite is equipped with electric and water hookups, a picnic table, lantern post, fire ring, and grill. There is a centralized bathhouse with restrooms, showers, and a coin laundry, along with a dump station near the campground entrance.

About the Authors

Sunshine Loveless is the founder and lead adventure guide of Outshine Adventures, an ecotour and travel company based in Chattanooga, Tennessee, that provides guided outdoor experiences, camper van rentals, and customized travel itineraries that encourage people to get outside, unplug, and connect with nature. Sunshine started the company in 2018 with just two paddleboards and an idea to get more people out exploring Chattanooga's scenic waterways. As the dream grew, so did the fleet of paddleboards and adventure offerings, to include other adventures like hiking, biking, yoga, and camping in a cool camper van. Sunshine is a gold medalist, cancer survivor, nature lover, adventure seeker, reformed raft guide, Kansan, and retired full-contact football player. They are happiest outside leading adventures and shines brightest when connecting others with nature and new experiences. You can follow their adventures on Instagram and Facebook at @outshine.adventures or visit their website (outshineadventures.com). Happy adventuring!

Growing up in a small, rural East Tennessee town, **Harold Stinnette** gained an appreciation for nature early in life. As a youth he spent many hours outdoors, fishing with his father or taking trips to the Smokies with his family. As he grew older he became more involved in hiking and camping and eventually developed a desire to record on film the beauty he saw in nature. Harold believes that nature photography is a positive way of learning to protect and preserve the natural world we all share. He is well known in Tennessee and throughout the Southeast for his exquisite images of nature and his love of the outdoors. He is a regular speaker at nature events and camera clubs. Sharing nature and nature photography through the teaching of nature photography workshops has been a passion of Harold's for many years. His images have been published in *Outdoor & Travel Photography*, *Birder's World*, and *Outdoor Photographer* magazines. His photographs have also been featured on postcards and in books and advertisements. Harold lives in Spring City, Tennessee, with his wife, Donna, and son, Brandon, where they own and operate Natural Impressions Nature Photography Workshops and Tours; their website is NaturalImpressionsphotography.com.